a delicate
fade

a delicate
fade

ben devries

MAR 3 1 2005

ZONDERVAN™

GRAND RAPIDS, MICHIGAN 49530 USA

ZONDERVAN™

A Delicate Fade
Copyright © 2004 by Benjamin J. DeVries

Requests for information should be addressed to:
Zondervan, Grand Rapids, Michigan 49530

Library of Congress Cataloging-in-Publication Data

DeVries, Ben, 1979–
    A delicate fade / Ben DeVries.— 1st ed.
    p. cm.
    Includes bibliographical references.
    ISBN 0-310-25535-X
    1. Christianity—Miscellanea. I. Title.
  BR124 .D48 2004
  230—dc22

                                        2003026644

Interior design by Beth Shagene

Printed in the United States of America

---

04 05 06 07 08 09 10 /❖ DC/ 10 9 8 7 6 5 4 3 2 1

to dr. Pate
for the only sense
I've ever made
out of life

contents.

p r e f a c e .

find me a song to sing
find me the words and a story I need
I could sing what I've always known
(find me)
I think I'm running out of time

and I'm scared to death of what I can't express
there's a word on the tip of my tongue
but it's already been said, I think
it's already been said before. (0.1)

it has been difficult to write the past few days. it was
difficult even before then. the last seven months were
the hardest I've ever been through and writing doesn't
help. it was always the things I couldn't say that I
needed to the most.

I've stared at this page with the poem at the top that
I've put through a hundred drafts, and I'm sick of staring

at a notebook I can only half-fill with the same words I used before, except rearranged, as if it would be better if I could edit myself.

sometimes it all seems cleaner and easier to read, and I think someone else might make it into a real book for me. but it's really never much better than the draft before or much different. and I could be enamored with the ideas of incompletion and imperfection and even try to write about them and still know that I can never let them be a part of this.

I've stopped and started over more times than I can remember, and I think that I like the times between the best because I feel the most whole then, as if I know what needs to be said, and almost as if I could write more of it next time. the need to express takes me over like it did a long time ago when I first knew I had to write. and I know I could never let this go until it is done.

I felt it again a moment ago, like I did yesterday, when I remembered something more than words. but it's never as strong as the inadequacy I feel every time I put my pen down and turn away (or the hurt I felt last night). I start to write and then catch myself because there's nothing I could say right now that comes close to what I imagined before, and what that was I have a terrible time remembering anyway. but I have to try.

I imagine that underneath all of this the need for release grows stronger and stronger, like forgetting and still being able to remember. I think that need must live in separate places, both on the surface and somewhere underneath where I keep it away from anything that could make it better. and if it does this must be why I always wrote to begin with.

when I was a boy I used to write about dinosaurs and other animals. I colored in black and white photocopies and drew big words that I took from library books and encyclopedias. sometimes I copied whole paragraphs word for word because that's all I could manage at the time, but I wanted them to be good.

I didn't write anymore until I grew up, and then I wrote about myself because I felt like I had lost it somewhere but at the same time my self was the only thing that never went away. I wrote songs to find it again and to figure out what was wrong with me. I didn't know how I could hurt so much or why I felt so confused.

I used to think it might be too late to write because I could never make sense of what had happened to me or where I am now. but I had to try because these thoughts were all that I had left and as awkward as they were and as simple as my words would be I needed to write them down and hope that someone else could find something beautiful in them.

I wrote a book about myself last summer, sort of a memoir but sad and vague more than anything else. I thought there was no point in stringing out a chain of details or experiences when they were only average and hopelessly boring. but I thought that maybe if I pieced them together just right I would find some hope in them and maybe someone else could read their own tears between the lines.

that's all I meant it to be, an answer and a strange kind of empathy, but it wasn't much of either one. the journals are in my closet somewhere with all the other things I used to write and think were important. but they don't seem so final now or so urgent. and some days I wish neither would this.

I wanted to write something different, something more than myself and more like beauty is supposed to be. it seems so small in all of this and I wish I could have captured more of it, but I don't think that I did. even if I did I don't know if I would see it anyway.

> reality and at once the deep, daily perceiving
> that reality is something distant that comes
>   infinitely
> slowly to those who have patience. (0.2, Rilke)

> while little hands make vain attempt our
> wanderings to guide. (0.3, Carroll)

one:
b e t w e e n.

not to take them out of the world, but they
do not belong to this world. (1.1)

some days I feel completely incapable of processing life,
and most likely I am. acknowledging this doesn't help as
much as I thought it would.

I've felt this way more often than I wanted the past few
months, and it probably goes back much farther than
that except I thought I had a better handle on things
then. maybe I did, or maybe I didn't know as much as
I do now, which is a funny thought because I still don't
know enough to make that much of.

life comes in bits and pieces to me. I wrote my thoughts
on little slips of paper when I began this so that I
wouldn't get confused. I thought I would remember them

that way and could put them together when they made more sense.

I put the good ones in the middle and arranged the others on both sides where they seemed to fit, all in a way that resembled balance. but together they seemed so much smaller and more confusing, and I threw most of them away because they weren't at all what I wanted to say.

I don't know what that was or if I'm doing any better now, but at least this is more than I said the last time. (mostly that I feel incomplete.)

I used to see every part of life as a separate incident, even the past and what I remembered as good. sometimes I would string parts together in a chain to see where the most recent one should fit, but it was always broken and awkward like the rest and I would always be disappointed when it couldn't.

once in a while I opened up a little more to see if something new and whole could fit inside what's left of myself. I wondered if it could make it better or make up for everything I missed, and I hate it when I think like this because I know it never can. the hole inside of me is too big to be filled, at least by something here, but sometimes I forget this because I need too much.

disappointment feels just like the first time every time, like getting used to emptiness but never being without the feeling of hurt. and before the new thing leaves, to try to make room for itself it makes the hole a little bigger until I don't think I could feel any more, until the next time. and then it's gone.

some days I feel life all at once, as if it was just waiting for me to come to in order to let me know that it was never life that hurt me but only something vaguely resembling that, something much smaller and incomplete. and if I should be afraid it should be now that I have wondered if I ever knew at all, or if this has all just been pretend.

maybe I've opened only little boxes of life and the smallest of them is me. maybe I didn't even open them so much as shake them gently to see if I could guess what was inside, and if the packaging tore at all I quickly wrapped them back up to put them safely on the shelf where they belong, or maybe to give them away.

the ones I'm not completely afraid to open I unwrap cautiously and stare at for a while, but with my eyes half closed because there's too much to see and I'm afraid of what it all might mean. and then I put them with the others.

I drew a picture of myself once. I erased it and then drew another of a boy in the shadow with a tear in his eye and something like the weight of the world on his shoulders. it seemed so sad and sometimes more than that, but I think I drew it because that was all I knew at the time and I couldn't look anymore.

I didn't know yet that the shadow was from the curtains around me and that the hurt I felt was as much from what I couldn't remember or understand as anything from the outside. I don't know quite what to make of this except that the picture is still a safer place than any other I know. and I should try to draw another of the place between where I am and where I used to be and hope it's not as dark as the last one.

I couldn't take another one of those.

I think that's what I've been feeling lately, an overwhelming whole and one so much heavier than I ever thought it could be. I thought it would be easier to manage by now, but it's still only a part that I see and not the whole. and I thought I held it for a moment, but it was only a moment.

even the pieces have become indistinct and more distant from each other. and I know this some days but I feel it more than anything else.

there is a field I pass by on my way home from work. it's not the field I will remember so much as thinking I could lie there one day where the corn used to grow and feel nothing but peace.

I would lie there with my arms and legs spread out in the mud and stare at the sky with only a few clouds to catch my interest. but mostly I would look in a calm sort of way unafraid of being interrupted and not think about anything at all, especially those things I've always wanted to let go.

I am so tired and so unable to handle all of this, but for one moment it's gone and all I know is happiness and something of peace. and it washes over me in a way that I never want to let it go and I wonder if I could take it with me when life moves on.

but it's just a moment after all, and soon it passes by like the field.

I thought I took a little more of it with me, but it's leaving that's always so difficult, and turning away. I wish I could hold it a little longer this time.

there are no words to describe feeling except the ones that come afterward, and they never really add up. I feel almost ashamed that all I can do now is tell how I wasn't able to hold on to the one thing that I needed to the most, or even keep it close. it must be difficult to explain why anyone would allow it to slip away, but I tried so hard to make it stay and I wish it would, but it doesn't.

it's so easy to get lost in words when there is so much more that needs to be said. some days I feel like I'm just rambling off the most basic thoughts because everything I've held to myself is everything I can't get out. it all seems so featureless and so far away, and all I can do is piece together the thoughts I can remember only separately. and this never amounts to what I needed it to be.

I used to love writing songs because it seemed so simple. find a chorus and a verse and give them a melody and a bridge. I could pick a line out of thin air, like the one that surprised me that I could think of it, or even the one that was more of dull aching than anything specific. and in the space of a few words I could find the perfect expression for something I could never have spoken out loud. and whatever was left unsaid was wrapped up somewhere in the harmony or in the way the lyrics were sung, and it was all somehow so much bigger than the song itself, which seemed so small.

I never knew that a book could be so big or have so much to say and still be so clumsy and so hopelessly inadequate. (but maybe it's just me.) there is so much room that I'm afraid I could never fill it with anything meaningful past my own assumptions and insecurities and the extremes on either side of them that might give some definition and stability.

I expected something of a mess and more bends in the path than I would know how to take. it's so hard to reach outside yourself and come back to the place you started from. it's not the same all of a sudden, and not the way you wanted to remember it.

but I never expected to be lost in the truth itself. I was looking for it, or something as close to it as I could manage, but it was as if the luxury of curiosity was ripped away before it was even allowed to exist and all that was left was something much more urgent.

I thought I had left this feeling of insecurity behind before I began, but I didn't. there is so much more to being hurt than I thought and more to being incomplete. I thought I was strong enough to reach past them and hold on to the reasons I had for believing that life is made of more. sometimes I think I was cursed for all the hell I've gone through just to reach for them.

my professor dr. Pate said that paradox is just a "study in contrasts" (1.2). every semester he scribbled his thesis on the board and it was almost as if a simple recognition of this could be the cure-all to difficulty. the paradox of the kingdom could be a kind of science with problems and equations, and an answer or a balance if you knew the right questions to ask.

we would have asked so much more if we'd known at the time, but it didn't seem so important then. I think he taught us mostly what was expected of a theology teacher at our school, with the conclusion before the question is even asked or felt, which is about as much as any of us can handle anymore. but it was never that simple for him.

sometimes he allowed himself to teach beyond what we could copy down and what could never be whole but only partial and broken because it touched his own life. and I found myself slowly for the first time and the world that I belong to and the part of truth that somehow might be able to hold me.

not that it was too fragile or too small to hold me before, but it was always me that was too simple and life that was too small.

"the poet has to work by analogies. all of the subtler states of emotion . . . necessarily demand metaphor for their expression. . . . metaphors do not lie in the same plane or fit neatly edge to edge. there is a continual tilting of the planes; necessary overlappings, discrepancies, contradictions. even the most direct and simple poet is forced into paradoxes far more often than we think, if we are sufficiently alive to what he is doing" (1.3, Brooks).

Aquinas said that nothing that implies contradiction could fall under the sovereignty of God (1.4). but I don't believe this. it might be the right thing to say if it weren't that *implies* is such a big word and *contradiction* didn't depend so much on it.

I don't think anyone would want tension, not when there is so much at stake. it's at least a discomfort and sometimes much worse, but I think we're more worried about contradiction in itself than whether it's any real challenge to God. I don't believe he is ever forced into or trapped by anything, but I don't think he's without the means to allow or to create curiosity either.

this must be one of the most human tendencies, to forget complexity or to make it go away because it's more than I can handle right now.

but sometimes it takes me when I'm not watching or ready to explain it away, and it wraps around me more than I can ever manage or want to admit, and almost as if it always was.

maybe Aquinas would have been surprised or maybe he meant something different, because I know I've always been within the reach of God but the consequences of these inconsistencies still won't leave me. and even paradox must be lost in the hands I can feel but don't always see, because it was me who implied there was a contradiction to begin with.

the only sense I ever made out of life was when a man told me the kingdom of God is placed between this world and the one to come. he said it hangs like a curtain between what I can see and feel (everything fragile and fading, like me) and everything whole.

as weak as I am and as blind, it's here waiting to show itself. and someday with or without me it will be complete.

and today as far as I will ever know it is perfect but not
yet (1.5, Cullmann). and all I ever wanted was to hold
this for a moment and know that I was home.

    there is a picture in the window, a faded image
        in the half-glow
    and I can see through this night line to the
        world outside
    but first this quiet falling on my mind, and a
        display of empty things
    I think I have forgotten how to dream
    and hope, maybe I remember what that means.

    there is a story in the white book, a vague
        memory in my notebook
    and I can see through the dead lines to the
        tears inside
    but first this silence pounding on my eyes, and
    a cascade of simple things
    I think I have forgotten what that means
        (maybe I remembered how to dream).

    a lifetime and I saw you, I can see you change
    I remember everything (except what I am now)
    I remember how I spent all this time looking
    a lifetime watching, but I lost myself
        somewhere
    I found myself between what is and what was
        meant to be. (1.6)

two :
    sorrow .

either the well was very deep, or she fell very
slowly. (2.1, Carroll)

I waited so long to write this part. it's strange that I
could be here now and not know what to say, but life is
often like that, especially when it comes to sadness.

you build the expectation for letting it go, and even
putting it to words becomes one last chance at empathy.
I don't expect so much from writing, or even from
listening, not like I did before. but there is still always
the strange compulsion to hope, and I don't know why
this is.

most everything I've written has been melancholic or
sad. I can write from disappointment or anger or even
from bitterness, but underneath it all is the same feeling

of loss I can never describe. I've tried but I feel like I am just repeating myself. and I don't mean to complain.

I've had to fight sadness more than I expected in writing this. I started out with so much hope and the potential to be objective about what came my way. but the more composed and intelligent I tried to be, the more I knew that I was only hiding from myself and whatever else I knew to be true.

philosophy is uncomplicated and safe. it's so much easier to write when emotion is buried under layers of pretense or something abstract because it's too subjective and vague to be part of the bigger picture, let alone seen as valid. but I never was able to forget about it.

they say to write what you know, and I wish more than anything that I could—everything I feel right now, everything I'm unsure of and everything I don't want anymore. it might be sorrow today or maybe something more damaging. but I could never write about that.

maybe tomorrow won't be so bad and it will turn out that I only made more of tonight than I needed to. I should go to bed and sleep it off because that's all I can do and hope to wake up feeling better.

tomorrow will be a good day until consciousness begins all over again. some days there is a slower build to consciousness and sometimes even a more promising delay, but it always comes back. in those moments when

I'm not quite awake, I hear the fan blowing softly and the air moving through the window, and the sense of urgency isn't so strong. I wish it could be different but it hasn't been as long as I can remember.

I told that to a friend once and he smiled as if it was a childish thing to say. I tried explaining it to him, but I gave up because he couldn't understand. I think he knows what pain is and maybe even doubt, but I don't think he knows despair.

if he did he would have said something much more empathetic, because despair isn't something you can smile or talk away.

it's awkward to begin with emotion when you're looking for truth. it's vague and quite possibly misleading, just like they warned me about experience. but when it's the one thing that never leaves me, even if it changes, I think it deserves a moment's notice, even if just as a question. I have to do something with it, and I don't know what else it might become.

even feeling has an end I think, but it comes so slowly.

existence is a strange thing. it falls under the surface, under all the things I throw on top of it until one day it's forgotten with everything else that used to be important, if only I could remember. it becomes an assumed separate reality if it's identified at all, not as important as tomorrow or what I will do with today. but it continues nonetheless beneath the life I think I am creating.

then one day it comes to the surface and becomes the one thing I can't hide from myself anymore (but still no one else can see). all the other layers have been pulled away or broken, and all that's left is the unbearable presence of existence with nothing to lessen it. it feels heavier than all of the distractions put together.

it is better to choose despair than expedients (2.2, Kierkegaard, Hannay). but I wonder if we ever really choose for ourselves until one of the two is offered to us. (you don't refuse a gift.) then even life itself can seem like a poor alternative to coping. it seems so small and so much of me.

I wonder if this is all my life is: a default survival and some days not even that. it seems different from what it was supposed to be and from what I asked for.

maybe I don't want it anymore.

Groeschel said the only question is whether we are going to be saved (2.3). I would agree, but it seems like the question has already been asked, and the stakes are so much more immediate than I thought.

Camus said that the only question worth asking is whether we should even stay (2.4), and maybe this isn't such a strange thing to ask after all. a simple yes or no would be good enough, but I never expected to be caught somewhere in the middle.

sadness is too often described from the outside looking in, as if it were exaggerated or as if pain and despair were nonpossibilities to anyone who doesn't have to deal with them personally. they try to excuse them away or give enough reasons why they were never valid in the first place. but to acknowledge that they are real and just as deep as I have made them out to be is more of an offense than even I could manage right now.

art never assumes that parts of life remain untouched by sorrow, at least not the art which I have loved. most of my life it was my only comfort when I felt alone because it never said that I shouldn't be hurting this much or that I should be in a better place.

I remember reading about van Gogh, how he tried to kill himself and then bled to death over the next several days while people went on living in the room below. the description of his death seemed so calm, like the time he cut his ear off, except they found him too late this time.

I wondered if I was reading a gothic story or the end of a biography and how a good man died. it was almost laughable the way it was all described, the lack of basic human empathy, and I wondered if somewhere in the story fate was laughing with us. but I imagined Vincent's eyes and the look in them that was hurting and tired but almost relieved that soon he wouldn't have to feel anything anymore.

and he isn't the only artist or lost soul whose experience could be described this way: a lifetime of hoping that beauty could absorb the pain that never goes away. we have our masterpieces and our collections, and they have a hole in their hearts where their dreams and their need were given away without so much as a word in return while they were alive.

no one speaks without hoping someone will listen.

there must be different ways of processing pain. we are able to recognize imbalance even in the ones we admire the most, and everyone who hurts differently than us is everyone who should pull themselves together. but it's when we see it in ourselves that it's most embarrassing and most desperately in need of defending.

Doctorow wrote that "the numbers [of pain] are exponential, we examine them one by one and they crush us in waves, and if we let them hurl us over ourselves . . . with their incredible breath-taking multiplicative fury we find only one at a time available to our comprehension" quietly staring us in the face (2.5).

there's a lake behind the apartment where I lived this past year, a small channel lake with pontoon boats and fishers in the summer and ice all winter long. I remember the open sky and the little beachfront leading to the steps and to my back door.

I've stood by the water so many times with an aching in my heart, or I would have felt the ache if I hadn't been so tired. some nights I catch myself hoping for the surprise of some relief or maybe just a half-hour's peace if there's to be no grand solution tonight. (sometimes I regret that there still is hope.)

some nights I meet God between the beauty and the void, and for those few moments all is right with the world. but some nights, and usually the ones when I need him the most, I find only more emptiness and I turn and walk away because I don't think I can take any more.

and I would rather hurt somewhere I can be alone.

I've lain on the floor of my apartment more times than I can remember, my face in the carpet and my legs curled up behind me, my hands groping for anything that could absorb some of the pain. but there is nothing. music plays softly in the background or sometimes heavily, but it's hollow like the room around me and the thoughts in my head. they aren't featureless so much as terribly plain, and I could scream them out but they've already been said and I would only wake the neighbors up.

I could call someone, but it's too late and I really can't right now. they've heard more than I wanted to say and

I've only felt worse for telling them. I rock back and forth like a baby waiting for someone to calm me, racking my mind for any shred of peace I might have forgotten or thrown away. but I don't think I will find it tonight.

"[the] raving madman, when nothing else
can ease him, charges into his dark night
howling, pounds on the padded wall, and feels
the rage being taken in and pacified" (2.6, Rilke).

I try to calm down, lie still for a minute and think of something simple to accomplish—a movie to watch or maybe something to eat. (he could be numb from all the reflection.)

I wonder sometimes if I ask for too much. I would give almost anything for just a touch, just one moment when I could feel a hand on my shoulder or arms around me letting me know that I am all right, that I am loved and that it could make a difference to me.

I don't think hope was ever meant for me. it's such a delicate thing to begin with and I could never hold it safe. but honestly I didn't try to let it go this time.

stare at the darkness long enough and the shadows become more featureless and the spaces between more blurred and gray, and the silence more offensive in its absence of response than anything you could feel in yourself. and I miss those times I cried and ran into the

smaller emptiness and remembered that someday change
could come.

"forgive me, I think I lost myself somehow
somewhere I should never be, I think I lost myself
when I was found, what did you mean that you
would never leave me alone?
I think I lost you somehow" (2.7).

Frankl wrote about "the crowning experience of all, for
the homecoming man, that, after all he has suffered,
there is nothing he need fear anymore—except his God"
(2.8). the fear of the Lord might be the beginning of
wisdom but it could also be the beginning of terror. and
I think this is what I've always been most afraid of.

I never really questioned the sovereignty of God. I never
thought that his reach was somehow cut short or that he
became helpless at a certain point. but it would have
been easier to believe this.

I did question God's goodness and whether he would ever
be good to me.

sometimes I still do. it's easy to doubt when his presence
is never seen except in everything that hurts. and some
days this is all life is made of. I used to think I was the
only one to feel this way, but I confused loneliness with
isolation, and I'm not so alone now.

it's awkward to question God or be angry with him when
we've been taught never to do this because it would

distance us from him. you never know when he might walk away for good. but it's not so hard when God is absent to begin with, and I hear a voice inside me say that as much as I've disappointed him I know I never could have deserved this.

it isn't so difficult to be angry when God is made to be the cause of all things, because whether he created all things or just allows them to happen, you feel the same pain and the same betrayal when everything good is taken away and replaced with everything dead and dying. and this is all I was left with, and mostly myself.

Aquinas said that "all things changeable and capable of defeat must be traced back to an immovable and self-necessary first principle" (2.9). and I know he must be right, except we decided a long time ago that life and sometimes even God can only originate or fit within the borders we identify or control.

but life doesn't fit inside this bubble of what I think should or shouldn't be happening, and neither does faith. but the God I know has always assumed complete control, regardless of what I think completion is or what I want it to be.

Job questioned God because he didn't understand him, and his friends defended what even God wouldn't defend, that faith is always answered with good and pain is only the result of evil. but God was silent about everything except that he exists.

I'm disappointed at how violently God answered Job when it was the others who deserved to be crucified for their lack of compassion and understanding. but maybe Job was the strongest of them at the time and God wanted to show himself most to him.

some days I hold on to sadness because it's my only comfort. it's there when everyone else goes away, and I'm lonely then but not as much as when they dismiss me when I need their empathy the most.

"why don't you listen?" they ask me. "why don't you understand like I do?"

and I sit and listen quietly to them until I can turn away, because I used to be angry but now I'm only more sad that they could never understand. it must be strange to be so adamant where God has been so silent, and I listen with my eyes closed to loud words that only sound mumbled to me as though repeated in a trance. most of all they sound tired.

"you seem so sad," I want to say back. "were you disappointed in me? did I hurt you? did I say something wrong? I can see the hurt on your face as though I said something bad, but I'm sorry. I never meant to be like this. I never meant to be afraid."

I try to explain it to myself to see if there's some reason
to believe I will get better and someone else could help.
I've always wanted to believe, but I never really do.
nothing ever changes. I think the hole in my heart is too
deep and it only makes me wish the outside would go
away.

there is so much I needed to say but I don't think it
came out right. I've fought so hard for balance. that's
what this was all about, after all. but I couldn't hold it
like I needed to.

I always wanted release more than anything else, and
maybe this is the closest I can come.

three:
beauty.

all this he knows, and he cannot but suffer
keenly from the sharp contrast between what is
and what ought to be. (3.1, Tolstoy)

I remember the times at school I hurt the most and how
I hid myself in a shell away from everyone who could
hurt me more. this seemed more real than anything else,
my self-contained world. but mostly it just kept what
already hurt inside.

I remember sitting alone in the cafeteria not long before
I left. students passed by to sit with someone else, like
usual, but one friend stopped and asked me how I was.
normally I wouldn't say too much but I told him I felt
like every other day except I couldn't hide it very well
today, and I felt I was just waiting for everything to get
worse.

as much as I try to remember what hope is, some days
I think I can never get it back. those moments I'm well
never last as long as I need them to and I quickly fall
back to where I've always been. maybe there's too much
behind me now to turn away.

my friend said I was like a candle in a dark place that
couldn't light a way out or see how beautiful its
existence had become. I never really looked him in the
eye because I was ashamed, but I thought I saw a tear,
and whether it was his or mine didn't matter as much as
something in what he said that reminded me of faith.

but I was too weak then to make it mine.

I never could see life the way he did, like the boy in the
movie who could never get enough of it. beauty existed

in a world separate from me and somehow he had found it but I couldn't. I recognized it sometimes but I didn't let it affect me because it hurt too much. it hurt because I never let it make any difference to me.

a year ago I sat in a bookstore coffee shop with a notebook and a magazine that had something to do with art or the movies. I'd spent the week before, or maybe the whole year, wishing I was in a different place, and some days wishing I were dead because it seemed like that would be more real than what was happening to me.

I'd sat there the night before and flipped the pages of a book to pass the time, then left to walk downtown and think of what would never change or maybe write another song. but I couldn't then because nothing mattered anymore. it never really helped anyway.

but today I saw a painting in the magazine and listened to a song I can't remember, and somewhere between the painting and the music and the thoughts in my head something came alive that said I wasn't the first to feel this way, something beyond expression but as close as I could come. it said that every part of me, and even the broken ones (I feel them the most), is both beautiful and sad. and I never knew before that it could be that way.

all of life is beautiful, whatever it is made of, because somewhere in this awful mess some things half but perfect can be found. and beauty found me when the only hope I had was in decay.

I never knew what to do with beauty until I realized it is made of sadness too. then it became more beautiful somehow because I was allowed to feel.

I don't know how to fix myself anymore. I thought I would have to be removed from everything that hurt before I could hope again. but I never expected hope to find me in the deepest part of pain and stay with me there.

hope has faded since then but it has never completely gone away.

all my life I've heard about salvation, how it can find us only when we need it most. I've heard about brokenness and how God can heal us only when we're breaking apart and small. I've known this but not that it would happen to me and not that it could feel so much like pain or that need could feel so much like despair.

brokenness was always made out to be much smaller and more defined and not that it could get out of hand or ruin a person's life. I'd thought I'd known it before, but I didn't really know what it was until things got so bad that it was hard to breathe or to wake up the next morning.

and I never knew that faith could be so incapable of fixing anything at all.

I've known sadness as long as I can remember. if it went away it came back stronger and seemed more final. off and on it became more serious and even God was absent, just like everything else that was good. nothing really changed about this, not even when I realized life might not always be this hard. (though something tells me that it always will be.)

I've struggled with this impression since the euphoria of beauty faded away and life didn't change. but I understand beauty better, if only a little, and I know that it's no different now than it was then, and nothing is more or less complete than it was before.

there's a song on an acoustic album by Nine Inch Nails that's maybe the best expression of existence I've ever heard (3.2). it begins with a simple melody and electronic hums, then moves on to a slowly building buzz that threatens to bury everything else but instead it fades away, leaving the melody to carry on peacefully a little while before it returns. and this happens over and over again.

but somehow those moments when the buzz and the melody come together are not so much moments of tension as resolution, as if they somehow complement and even complete each other.

and I want this to be true.

the song ends the same way it begins but with a sound like a human voice. and whether it's a muffled scream or a longing drone I'm not quite sure. but I think either one would be fine.

each time I listen I feel as though I'm hearing not just a song but something more familiar, and maybe even existence as it might be. it isn't often that tension and peace belong together, but when I listen I know beauty and I know rest and only because they're made of sadness as much as anything else. you can't listen to the rest of their music and not know this is true.

any other time tension is a distraction or a disruption of anything whole, but here for five minutes it's only perfect. I play the song over and over, but the feeling lasts only as long as it takes the hum to fade away and I know it's time to move on to what is real. but reality seems so much less aesthetic because the contrasts are more prolonged and intricate and I don't see all of their parts.

harmony always comes to an end and when it does I'm left only with a residue and the longing for it to come back. some days this desire is unbearable, and some it's just awkward, and I can't remember when hope was any different.

when I was a boy life was simpler. questions were smaller and easily answered, and the ones that were confusing I never thought about too long because I figured they were meant for me to deal with when I grew up. but they never bothered me too much. not like they do now.

maybe I remember a simple life because I've lived the more complicated one so long I just assume the opposite must have been true at one point. life can't be complicated unless it can be simple too, otherwise where did I get the idea of complication from? I could have made it up, but why would I do that when I've fought it my whole life? I've always thought I was supposed to, especially when it wasn't safe.

I never wanted to stay where I could be hurt.

maybe I don't exaggerate innocence so much as remember what I wanted it to be. Lewis said we romanticize the past by remembering only what was good about it (3.3). and I know that he was right. but there must be something else to it as well.

I remember baseball and insects and best friends. I remember feeling happy and being loved and I think I knew more of what contentment is. we never had much money or much of anything our own, and though this was only a temporary disappointment and didn't mean that much to me, I was a dreamer in more important ways as well.

hurt was more immediate and came in smaller incidents that I quickly put behind me. (except for one.) but I knew what it felt like to be made fun of and not belong.

I remember quiet places and places where it seemed strange that I would be the only one. I would sit alone under a rack of clothes in a store or in the park just down the street, and I thought when I was bigger I would understand how I could be alone when there was so much life around me.

when I was a little older I felt the same awkwardness, except that it was endless and much more damaging. five years passed without anything but rain and gray skies, and I biked to school every morning in wind so strong that I stood on the pedals and was hardly able to move. I could have cursed God for allowing such a dismal world to exist.

and it never ended.

day after day the rain never stopped, and when I came home I was even more tired and alone. I remember the clouds most of all and the wet brown brick streets for what they did to me. I hated them and everything about this place that hurts you even when you're already dead and even when you're gone.

there was nothing good about a pain that never went away, except that it was all of me and I grew used to it, and I took it with me when I left. it was the only consistency I ever had. after every change I would look back and miss where I had come from, but I knew it wasn't any better there. maybe it helped me feel less disappointed, or maybe it helped me make the bad memories good. or maybe I remembered the past for what it could have been if only I had known that it was home.

it's easier to find beauty looking back, like goodness and truth. but it's more difficult to see it today (if less nostalgic).

"all that we call common sense and rationality and practicality and positivism only means that for certain dead levels of our life we forget that we have forgotten. all that we call spirit and art and ecstasy only means that for one awful instant we remember that we forget" (3.4, Chesterton).

they say that beauty bears the mark of truth. I think real beauty must be only the kind that we aren't able to control or tame. otherwise it would be something we had made for ourselves and much less beautiful.

and it wouldn't be able to know us.

there is a dignity to sorrow that could only create itself or come from something higher. sometimes I can step outside myself and see it, but most of the time I can't. and even so it must still be there. I didn't make this or want it, but it's a strange gift.

true beauty can be terrifying, especially the closer it comes to home or when we try to capture it. dreamers dream the biggest nightmares and maybe this works the other way around as well.

van Gogh painted what he knew and what was beautiful, but it wasn't what other people saw. he painted old women in peat fields and miners coming home from work. he used bright colors and colors that were only different dirty shades of gray. and he put them all on canvas as if he couldn't contain them any longer, but they were all beautiful to him (3.5).

sometimes I think he must have seen what God sees, but then he shot himself. (maybe this isn't so strange.)

as small as we are, there's madness in embracing reality as it is. glimpsing anything beautiful or eternal in existence would be not only clumsy but terribly frightening, not only because it's a strange concept but because I don't know where to put the piece of beauty where it won't hurt me when it leaves.

Kierkegaard thought the only real despair is in realizing we're caught somewhere between the finite and the infinite. anything imperfect that found any part of the ever-complete within its reach but still so far away would feel only a tearing between the two that the self could never process or get past (3.6).

"anxious, we keep longing for a foothold—
we, at times too young for what is old
and too old for what has never been" (3.7, Rilke).

those moments of tension between acknowledging eternity and not grasping it are strange, because I know I never could've asked them to exist, but they're more beautiful than I ever could have imagined.

I'd give everything (even keep all of it) to experience them again. I seem to spend most of my energy trying to re-create them, as if somehow they're incomplete until I can find them again and put them where they won't be lost. if I could lock up beauty it might not seem so far away and maybe some days it would even feel like it was mine.

(I feel so ugly sometimes.)

I spend my waking life trying to reclaim the feelings of eternity and acceptance I felt at the same time once. I wish they would last longer. I wish I could capture them and bottle them up so I would never forget, like playing a song by Björk over and over just to hear the chorus of angels at the end. for those few seconds I'm taken to the place I know I will belong to someday when all of this is made better. but it must be somewhere here as well.

if imagination is the doorway to the eternal (3.8, Kierkegaard), the opening must be made of desire just as much. reality seems more transparent and emptier now, but this is where I am and where I'm home, at least today. and if it's beautiful in sorrow, it must be beautiful in loss somehow as well.

four:
    what is.

and we: spectators, always, everywhere,
turned towards the world of objects, never
    outward.
it fills us. we arrange it. it breaks down.
we rearrange it, then break down ourselves.
    (4.1, Rilke)

most of my short existence I've thought that there were
things and maybe even whole worlds outside of my
perception, but I always let them stay where they were
and where they couldn't bother me so much.

if you acknowledge something I suppose you have to
interact with it and let it affect you in some way. but if
the thing turns out to be unsafe and you let it in too far
to protect yourself anymore, you feel almost like a fool
for ever having acknowledged it to begin with.

I could have kept the unknown away and never felt any of this. but then I would have existed only in some other place where I wouldn't have recognized it at all, except for the part that hurt me somehow. and that isn't a very happy place to be either.

46 "to exist alongside the frightening unknown is often simply intolerable. in order to cope, we all need some comprehensible grasp of events outside our control, whether or not the interim explanations turn out to be true" (4.2, Shenk).

most of what I know is divided into areas that are separate from each other. they are sectors with boundaries that either I've made or have been made for me and that I should hold to.

life as it is or as it was meant to be (sometimes I don't see much difference) is easier to adapt to than to recreate. so I find the niches that work best for me and that are always easiest to manage and I make them my very own.

but sometimes something outside finds me and I'm lost in the awkwardness or terror of whatever it might be. but all along it knew me and was close to me.

"either we climb down into the abyss willingly with our eyes open, or we risk falling into it with our eyes closed" (4.3, Buechner).

some days as much as I'm afraid of what life or God could do to me, I'm just as afraid of what I could do to myself.

I spend much of my life trying to defend what I've become. whatever I feel and need the most is what I believe is real and build a wall around. and I describe it as best I can to convince someone else that it's valid and to give myself reasons to exist this way.

(it's the only way I can.)

I must have done the same with this. I'm afraid that everything I've said is what I needed it to be and whatever truth I've written down is what I've made up for now and not what it will be someday when I am more complete. maybe it's completely meaningless now.

but I hope I'm not so much defending myself (I might be, but I don't really like myself) as trying to find the place I do belong. I want to find a place where truth is more than what hurts me and where I can grow and get better like I always wanted to, and maybe even where I can rest.

I've heard that some people are never content unless they're fighting themselves (4.4, Groeschel), and I wonder if I am like them. I wonder if I will ever be at peace or if I will always go through life in the fog and the mud, crawling inside myself at every bump. I tend to take things hard, as if each fall is the last word and I can never get back up.

all this could be just a reaction to another collapse. I thought I had something more positive to say when I got started, but it feels like I'm just digging a deeper hole to climb out of.

sometimes I wish I could walk away, by some fluke put distance between me and myself. I would turn and see myself from a different place and for one moment I would see more than the pieces I have collected and the pictures I have imagined, and I would see something of the bigger world which is around me and which I'm only a tiny part of.

it must be difficult to describe something outside of yourself. I wonder if I ever really could.

as hard as I try to look past myself, my eyes and my mind still filter everything I take in. and if I am able to leave myself for just a moment I've only created another reality separate from me, and it would be better to know myself than to do that.

my perception of childhood or the times I found myself again is just as framed and colored in as I need it to be. no matter how well I think I understand what really happened it's still little more than just the silhouette I need to make sense of things and to cope with today.

some of what I remember might be part of a bigger picture, but not all of it. I find some peace in bringing everything I've felt under one umbrella of purpose or meaning. and I do the same with what I'm experiencing today, except that right at this moment it's much more difficult to recognize my own misperception. it's easier to realize misunderstandings looking back.

the more I am aware of the misperceptions I've had and keep them away from me, the more I need the ones that are left to continue on.

I remember being lost in a strange place, wondering why everything I knew was taken away from me. things seem much more final when you are little, and what I had left behind I couldn't even identify except in the smallest of things like baseball games and Skittles. the feeling of loss was overwhelming and I knew that what was taken away was something I couldn't replace, but I desperately needed to return to where I could still try to get it back again.

I heard someone in a movie say that "all of life is a coming-home" (4.5, *Patch Adams*). when I hear it now it makes me warm inside to think that I could still come home someday. I used to think that it was only on the other side of the ocean and that to go back for good was the only thing that mattered, I missed it so much.

we went home for a visit twice in five years, and each time it was both different from what I remembered and somewhat the same. I knew that I was changing more than the place I used to belong to.

the last time we went home I stayed because I knew that if I left again it wouldn't be there anymore and I could never come back. as awkward as it was, it was still better than being somewhere else. somewhere else was way too much like being abandoned and being nowhere at all.

I used to think of faith as a catchall for reality. I thought that if you put yourself in the position of salvation and what the Christian life was supposed to be you would be saved from all things, especially the ones that hurt. but I don't think faith is so much an umbrella as a hand underneath me that lets me feel everything that rains down. and it holds me when I can't feel any more and when I think I've left it for the pain and the questions.

I'm not sheltered or enclosed but exposed on every side. and I know this must be for a reason but I don't know what it is. sometimes even the sensation of falling seems not to be held back at all, and this could be just a feeling too but it's the hardest to understand.

faith would be a relief if it could take away the feelings of abandonment and death. but I feel like something worse is always waiting for me, something it will never help me be less afraid of.

they gave me a book to read. I've read it before but the words that were supposed to make me feel better only make me feel more alone and it's almost insulting to think I should hurt less for reading them.

I've tried enough to know I read only the verses that give me hope for what I've lost. and I can always look back and realize I was a fool for ever wanting what I did and thinking faith would help me get it, but somewhere in the mess of desire and insecurity there must have been a shred of human dignity and real need. and I always wondered how it could be so difficult to answer this.

false hope leads only to disappointment (and shame). but I could never let myself be angry with those words because I held on to them when I shouldn't have and believed in something that wasn't meant for me.

I don't think perception is cured by faith any more than anything else is. I used to think that it didn't exist or that it might not be so disconnected from reality if I believed hard enough. but the inconsistency between what is real and what I believe has always been more than I wanted it to be. and where this leaves me I'm not always sure.

perception begins with what you know, and what I know is so concocted already that adding to it wouldn't necessarily be a good thing. more than likely I would only have more reasons to protect what I already thought was true, and this was only meant to be a place to start from, even the book said that.

I remember church as a place with carpeted pews and a small balcony where I used to play after the service at night. I remember coffee and potlucks in the gym, and flowers behind the pulpit and in the foyer where I saw the people I knew. Sunday school was a class with felt pictures and Bible quizzes that I looked forward to more than the sermon afterward. but it turned into youth groups that met in basements with old couches and beanbag chairs and posters on the walls, and I knew I didn't belong there anymore. and I didn't want to.

when I was little I imagined God was a bright presence behind the clouds and then I didn't imagine him at all. I used to think he had a hand that reached through the lights as if lost and if it found me it would have to be uncomfortable because I couldn't imagine what it would feel like, but later I just knew that it would hurt. in pictures Jesus had a beard and a clean white robe and an odd look on his face that made him seem friendly but absent and lonely as if he lived in a different place too. but it seemed to work with the painting.

the songs we sang and the things we said became the heritage of our family and everyone like us. I didn't recognize it then and it didn't make sense for years. faith had nothing to do with the parts of me that haunted me the most except to add to them or to cover them up as if they didn't matter as much as I knew they did. but this was my home and where I was meant to be.

perception can come from being taught or from watching, usually a combination of both. sometimes it comes from drifting in a pool of everything unresolved and having your previous perceptions destroyed because they weren't whole enough keep you from drowning.

it can be shattered instantly or stretched out indefinitely. sometimes it feels like the stretching will never end and the moments between seem like places where security is just a cruel joke, and I'm waiting to come tumbling down in them as well.

I feel tired sometimes. life can be daunting in itself aside from the deeper themes of sorrow and every other one. I'm surprised by how much the everyday can consume and overwhelm me. I was so caught up in surviving the bigger catastrophes that I wasn't prepared for the smaller ones that would take their place. but sometimes this is all life is.

I wish it could be more than that, but it's not. I feel as if I'm functioning at a funeral home, whether as curator or a guest doesn't really matter. I stick to myself and stay quiet because it is required of me, but it seems as though there are important things we should be talking about now.

reality is absurd and seems mostly out of balance, and you would almost have to look away or embrace it compulsively to function with any amount of sanity. they say that insanity is repeating the same thing that didn't work the first time, so I'm not sure if it's stability we're trying to protect or something else.

"my reflection on life altogether lacks meaning. I take it some evil spirit has put a pair of spectacles on my nose, one glass of which magnifies to an enormous degree, while the other reduces to the same degree" (4.6, Kierkegaard).

54

I would desperately like to be happy (not just for my sake). but there's so much that beats around inside my head that I don't think I could ever let go until I know what I was supposed to learn from it. I think happiness must be for people who are not like me. I ask them how they can smile so much and they don't seem to have an answer for me, unless they don't want to tell me why. but I assume they must have forgotten it.

life is all about pretending or turning away. naivete is a helpful tool. ignorance might be too strong a thing to say, but whether either is chosen or acted out unwillingly isn't so important as what I do with them when I know that they exist. to use either one as an excuse to continue on the same way (some things will never change) is like saying I'm content not to wake up this morning and see what the new day will bring. even if it only brings rain, at least it's something real.

innocence is bliss, but isn't that what growing up is for? to replace it with the ability to cope with life as it really is? the perception of randomness that we're so proud of would be much more comforting if I didn't realize that I play such a big part in forming it. there must be others who are like me too, and then there is the one who holds all of us.

he can do so much, but I don't think it's ever random or dependent on my actions. I might perceive it as random, and even my choices might be based on this assumption, but what's so difficult to accept about this? why do I have to defend the logic of it to myself or anyone else? I'm only extending the awareness of my incompletion to the part of me that doesn't understand what it means to understand. and whether this is my heart or in my mind, I should know by now.

but it's easy to forget.

there's a theory that says a work of art is good only if all of its elements relate perfectly to each other. whatever doesn't fit is what doesn't belong and what isn't artistic.

ugly and bad and sometimes even wrong become what I don't know or what I don't understand more than concepts opposite of good. and I know this because it's always what I assumed was true and not because I know it is. this is where I think I am safe and where I have sheltered myself, but it's really only where I am least vulnerable and most afraid of what something unknown could do to me.

moral boundaries can be just a safeguard against what could hurt me. sometimes they are only the fabrication of my assumptions anyway and the inhibition of anything beyond my control, good or bad. I can be afraid of something I know, but I'm much more afraid of everything I don't know. and I will do anything to keep it that way, even make it mine in some unconscious or guarded sort of way.

acknowledging God as he is (as close as we can come to understanding him) is supposed to be the one entry into wisdom. we think he might be open to different choices or outcomes so we can avoid what would be difficult to accept and what would hurt us. but God must smile at this.

I saw a boy with crutches who seemed happier than I'll ever be, and I thought this was strange because he could never ignore his pain.

I am so tired of everything being half. I thought when I wrote my story out a year ago I could find some kind of answer to why I feel like this. but the ending came and went and it was more of a stopping place than a conclusion, and life went on without caring too much what I made of it. the same questions came back around as half-answers, half new faces. and I thought it would be easier this time, but it's almost harder for having been through it all before and never having left it behind.

life wouldn't disappoint me so much if I didn't disappoint myself. I set expectations that can never come true, especially for myself and the things that are closest to me. I wish I could accept less, but as much as I grow and try to, I never really can. sometimes I feel like I'm never even given a chance to be human.

I could learn to live with imperfection if it learned to live with me, but I don't think it can.

I wanted to be a zookeeper when I was little, or a baseball player. when I got older I just wanted to be somebody and I wanted to be loved. the first would have been easier. the last has only been a nightmare.

I was going to be in a band because maybe I could write and play a song about myself and be accepted for that. but if it happened now I think it would be too late to make a difference.

it's easier to love than to be loved because it's safer, and I never got back what I needed anyway. most people are glad to know that someone else is just as insecure as them and wants to listen to their problems. but they would rather keep me at a distance (just like I would like to keep myself) because otherwise they might allow themselves to realize how some issues run much deeper than the surface.

the best things about me are the broken ones. I didn't want it to be that way but I hold them out in front of me now like an identity. it's better than being someone I never was able to be, but I still fall just as hard. a house of cards built on rock is still a house of cards, and the foundation that was supposed to be there from the beginning seems more content to remind me of how weak I am than to be what it always should have been.

I thought stability was something that was waiting for me someday. I kept waiting and hoping but it never showed up. then I thought I must be responsible for creating it myself. but even what I built up removes itself bit by bit until there is nothing left at all. I can't stand on my own any longer and then I collapse. it used to be because of rejection and then failure, and then it was because of despair.

there must be different ways of processing incompletion. you could ignore it or make it out to be something smaller, or you could make it the end-all of experience, or anything in between. the first would be easier and make you happier, but the second can be a comfort too. and everywhere in between is probably what I'm dealing with right now.

resignation has a strange way of working itself out. apathy is a more subtle version of paranoia or depression, which I think I am more used to. but melancholy is an extension of all of them.

apathy isn't always a choice so much as a natural reaction. after attempting for the hundredth time to make things right with myself and the world around me, I know it's better to walk past now and take myself with me than to stop and try again. that way I won't be disappointed anymore. it's always me who does the changing, and maybe this is a good thing but it hurts too much.

sarcasm must be the easiest expression of tension. it can become an entire way of communication, for better or for worse, but I mostly use it to cover up what I know isn't right. I can use it on myself and laugh my defects away like they were doomed to absurdity from the beginning. but I think I am hiding a deeper fear that there is something wrong with me that won't ever be fixed.

the desire for completion produces odd results. I can try to recognize them and prevent myself from making the same mistakes again, but most of them are habits that won't go away.

we spend most of our lives pursuing the things we think will make us whole. but when we find them they're not what we want them to be. the realization of this is anticlimatic or even just the doorway to looking all over again for something slightly more revised. I don't see why it should be any different with faith.

Zen philosophy says that everything we take in is just a surface reality. I believe this might be exaggerated, because some things do exist as they are, but we forget that there are layers of perception between us and things. objects are different than they seem, mostly emptier and more lifeless because they can't give me what I need. passions and virtues could bring me happiness, but even they leave me sad and alone. and I wonder if it was better to hold on to the lesser things.

beauty on some level is only a surface layer (4.7, Huxley), and it hurts the most to realize this. it was only a window to the things I long for after all, and not the things themselves. it's only half of the picture and the rest is on some other side I haven't come to yet. I can get closer but I never feel it completely.

I like sad things and sad art because I don't expect so much from them. the things that make me happy are the things that scare me the most too. I wait for them to end or change into something I'm not able to process anymore. and no amount of experience can prepare you for the fearfulness of hope.

I see something I know I need and I watch it from a distance to see if it could be different from the ones before. sometimes I can still manage to break the barrier between need and fear by approaching it awkwardly to see if it could want me too, and this is where I fall.

they say not to expect completion from anything or to depend on anyone else to make you whole. and I know this, but I don't think it could mean not to expect anything at all because that would almost be inhuman.

as much as I know not to hope anymore, some desires
only get stronger the more I push them away.

I wonder how God could allow us to want so intensely
just to keep it from us every time we get close. there
seems to be a curse on whatever I need the most, mostly
reflecting back on me. and I don't know why it has to be
this way.

Tennyson said it's better to love and be hurt than never
to love at all (4.8). it also must be better at least to be
able to contemplate the idea of love or some other
beauty than never to experience it at all. a desire
unfulfilled is a terrible thing, especially when there is no
end to it. but it can't be as bad as not needing at all.

"to want rightly, on the other hand, is a great art,
or rather, it is a gift. . . . then, wanting is far more
profoundly significant than usual; . . . since the
latter really thinks of wanting in respect of what is
not, not in respect of what is" (4.9, Kierkegaard).

I've always been told that God is what I need the most,
that only he can fill this hole inside of me. but it keeps
getting bigger and more removed from the rest of life,
and even he doesn't seem to want to be there when I
need him the most.

the difference between what I know and what I feel is
sometimes large and sometimes very small. I can feel
something that may or may not be, but at the moment
it's never any less real to me. the difference between

perception and truth, or between good and bad motivations, is never really clear, but if I could at least identify all of them I might not be so numb to the endless struggle. I don't want what is less, but I don't know that what is more is good. sometimes I don't trust it at all.

if this is where change takes place (if change is for the better), then no matter the wrenching I could find some contentment here. if change comes slowly or if it comes hardly at all, it wouldn't matter because this is where I need to be.

I used to think there might be someplace safer, but there isn't.

if real truth exists, it must be big enough to hold all of this and make good come of it. and not just the parts I have identified or the conflicts I experience but everything else as well, because anything less would be something that's already failed.

truth as a whole disappoints, but because it's just that, whole. I don't see all of it or what it would mean to me.

five:
    and what could be.

and the truth will set you free.

the awkwardness of design merges with bizarre observation in the studies of beings. (5.1, van Gogh)

if I couldn't walk away then this must be what I'm left with. I could turn the other way, but it would still be me. 63

no matter how pure truth might be or how separate from all of this, it must still be connected somehow to me and my existence to be of any real meaning (to me). truth, even absolute, would be tied to a setting that appears changeable to me, and then of course to me, which could hardly be considered stable.

I don't even trust myself, let alone what something else could do to me. truth could find me, but what would there be to find? if it changed me or my environment, what exactly would it be changing, the perception I have of them or what they are in themselves?

if truth changed anything at all, it would first have to take away what is shallow or pretend before it could affect anything real. and I would probably feel this as terribly painful, maybe even intentionally cruel, because it takes away from everything I know.

"'nothing my father and I have made is ever wasted', he said quietly" (5.2, Hubbard).

when I was smaller and everything changed, it seemed like everything I lost was held out in front of me like a mobile over a baby. I saw the little stars suspended with the moon and the clouds, and the pictures they threw up on the walls. I lay there alone waiting for someone to reach in and hold me, but they never came. and the shapes and the shadows dangled in this dark place and never went away.

sometimes I saw a hand above me replace one shape with another, and I was afraid of it until it didn't seem so strange anymore. I kept on waiting for the hand to find me too, and some days I was angry that it didn't and some just sad, but I always felt alone.

he said to let the little children come to him, and I thought I did, but he wasn't there. I asked him to be, and sometimes when I made myself good I thought he might be, but usually he seemed far away.

Lewis said that the "creature's illusion of self-sufficiency must, for the creature's sake, be shattered" (5.3). but this doesn't make sense to me because I never thought I was able to save myself. maybe I expected salvation to look like something else, or dependency to be much easier than I wanted it to be.

part of the discrepancy might be that we identify introspection or self-consciousness with something unhealthy, like self-centeredness, and not with something that could bring us to a deeper insecurity. I'm not sure that self-centeredness is even an extension of self-consciousness, because self-centeredness seems to be based more on a false ideal of who I am. and self-awareness only gives me more reasons to like myself less than I already do, but at least I know a little better what I am dealing with.

I could look at myself forever and still not know completely.

sometimes I feel like I was put down in front of a mirror and told to stay there until I learn whatever I need to, no matter if I want to or not. and I stare at my reflection like a child stares at a tv screen, but the image is fuzzy, like the bad reception of a tv show I used to watch but don't remember completely. I try to look away because I see everything that makes me more afraid, but an unfiltered mirror is more than I can process right now.

introspection can be dangerous if it runs too deep, but it's just as unsafe when it's hardly begun at all. I could dig just deep enough to confront myself with something I already can't manage or understand. and if I come so far that I'm unable to turn away, I might be destroyed, but it would be a never-ending destruction.

the dark night of the soul may be more than just one night, and it might even be more than the different traumas coming together with my inability to cope with them, but it could be my own self falling apart (5.4, Groeschel).

healing is distant and something I associate with answers to surface questions and not with what I need to make it through tonight. I so much long to be free from the burden of being me, but freedom from myself is not what I thought it should be. it's more the creation of a separate identity that requires more effort to hold up than if I were to keep myself.

Buddha said that I could give my self away or even deny that it exists, and Christianity has said almost the same thing. but whatever it is I want to reach outside myself means nothing unless it's really me that finds it, or me that it finds. and if it's somewhere inside of me I should know myself well enough by now to know that it's still separate from me.

whatever is a part of me I can't lose without hiding in some way that I never really lost it or replaced it. and usually it's somewhere in all of this that I lose what I need most.

I don't want myself, and I could never support myself either. every person needs to establish their identity in something else (5.5, Pannenberg). and that something that accepts their identity must be close enough to hold it up without assuming it completely, otherwise what would be the purpose of individuality? I realize that this is not an eastern concept, but neither is being separate.

if something is complete in and of itself and is able to extend itself however much it wants or needs, what would be the point in creating separate entities only to absorb them at some other time? any contribution we could make to that being would be ruled out because we are broken and imperfect, and it could create much better extensions of itself.

but if there is meaning in relationships between persons, then God's purpose would be to create an environment and a salvation designed for us to relate back to him. I don't think that he needs this. and I wonder sometimes if what he created was the best of available options, but it must be what he wanted as far as I can tell.

he must have wanted a relationship with us very much to allow a situation that would hurt not only us but also himself. to a degree he sacrificed good and he sacrificed himself, unless even in this it was only for the purpose of receiving something much better back. maybe even God learned something more of himself, something that couldn't be known even by knowing everything, something of love or maybe trust.

I've heard we were created with a need inside of us for something more. but I thought we were created perfect and without need, and maybe that's the problem. we could know God as our creator or overseer, but never as our real friend or father, because there was nothing that compelled us to that except for a sense of attachment, and this is the making of innocence but not necessarily of a mature relationship.

in our perfection we were incapable of relating to him as he wanted. not that he made a mistake in this. and it's not that somewhere in our destruction and re-creation we would recover our completion, because it never existed to begin with, but that we would find it for the first time.

"I took you home, set you on the glass
I pulled off your wings then I laughed . . .
I've watched you change
like you never had wings" (5.6, Deftones).

Augustine said that "from its very start, the race of mortal men has been a race condemned" (5.7). you could say that we've been doomed to pain as well, and I have often said as much. the reality of both can't be denied or excused away. those on both sides of the fence have tried and failed, and not just because we are too small to understand the realities but because we never allowed ourselves to believe that they could be intended by the one who created our longing for good. I don't believe they're mutually exclusive anymore. I believe they're only even possible together, at least here.

the state of most things since the beginning would seem to deny the existence of any perfect creation. sometimes we look past this and assume it must be hiding somewhere and that we could find it again someday if we tried hard enough. but this isn't possible (even humanism should know by now) because we know ourselves, well enough at least.

if reality was meant to be the gateway to the kingdom, it has been difficult to find. God help us if his kingdom has become the American or the western church, because it must be very small. the Roman church thought it captured direct access to heaven under Constantine, and the state of truth has seemed to be horribly disfigured ever since and even defeated. and I wonder where God is in all of this, or if he is at all. it certainly is an awkward thing what he has allowed to continue.

even the cross seems like a grandiose failure. if it was supposed to be the salvation of all mankind, I don't think there have been too many saved. and if there were I'm not sure they always knew what from.

Freud wrote that we have always had two instincts, toward life and toward death. "our views have from the very first been *dualistic*" (5.8). but what if the two came together in a strange impulse both to reach for something better that could be waiting for us and to carry with us what is already broken?

then life would be what I am reaching toward and death would be what is taking place inside of me. and if salvation is more than an initial happening or a foregone conclusion at some future point and is also a constant going-on, then this motive toward death and toward life would also make sense.

salvation is often presented as a happy thing, but that would be the aftereffect and not the saving itself. if salvation really is a removal from something, but the removal is purposely incomplete, then the pulling itself would be indefinite. and it's never a very happy thing to be torn but never separated.

I could be removed from a difficulty or maybe even from myself, but never from the weakness itself. I want to leave and be taken someplace else.

"who do you say I am?" Jesus asked, but don't tell too many others if you think you know because they couldn't understand. the kingdom dawned with the coming of a messiah, but with a manger and a mass murder, and a kiss of betrayal and a cross with nails. and all this would have been pointless if it weren't for the good that he accomplished here on earth, but even this he told people to keep quiet about as if it wasn't that important. not nearly as much as what was in store, even if it was an apparent failure.

and he hung there asking why he was forsaken too, when he gave himself away because it was asked of him, knowing what would happen if he did.

sometimes I imagine him with his arms stretched across a beam of wood, on a hill where he would face every element and every torment, and he could do nothing at all except stay there and allow it to come. the greatest hurt of all must have been knowing how much he gave and how it would be rejected or made into something less: a quick fix at a revival or some social abnormality, but never what it really was.

the book says he died so we could live, and not our false selves, because they could never be worth dying for, but maybe the part of us somewhere below that still holds the image of what he made.

they said that he was a perfect man and still "complete in what is ours" (5.9, Ware). God was with us as one of us, and a day never went by that he didn't remember where he had come from or what he had become.

Lewis mentioned the concept of a *numinous,* an eternal being which in itself is beyond the ideas of good and bad. a connection could be made between them and it, but not necessarily, because something whole wouldn't by default associate with something less, even if it had created it. but the connection was made in the person of Christ because he associated himself with the problem of incompletion (even our rejection of good), and even to the point of death (5.10).

God chose to be affected by a weaker existence, and because of this he somehow suffers with us. Buechner said he "is never safe from us" (5.11), and I don't think this would be possible if he had not allowed himself to feel what it's like to be partial too, and to at least be tempted by the consequences associated with it.

it was said that our image (of him) was disfigured in the fall, and of course it was. but the image could never have been complete to begin with because we weren't like God, and this was what he intended, for us to be like him.

in the middle of the garden he put the tree of the knowledge of good and evil. and the serpent told Adam and Eve that if they were to eat its fruit they wouldn't die but they would become like God. and when we ate we began not only to know good and evil but to feel them in a way that only created beings could. I think God must have always known what we would choose, and in some way it must have been his design (5.12, Calvin).

of course, all that needs to be said is that if God does purpose all things, and all things for good, then our fall and degeneration must also fit under this umbrella, awkward as this may be. and the fall was meant not just for me but for all of reality, and all of it would be the environment in which it was meant for me to lose myself and to find myself again for the first time.

but I'm not sure if I can wait any longer to be complete.

"no, don't say that. who are you, a mere human being, to criticize God? should the thing that was created say to the one who made it, 'why have you made me like this?'" (Rom. 9:20).

at any point in history God could have decided that our development was completed and to restore a perfect state, but he didn't. and that moment of perfection is still waiting at some future point, and why at that time instead of any other I'm not sure. but every trial has an end.

reality may be incomplete, but it isn't what it is by default. even the tension between the kingdom as it really exists and as it was intended to be is never resolved for now beyond accepting it for what it is.

if God allowed an environment to exist in which I would be presented with myself and also something of what I am supposed to become, it might be possible, even in the inconsistency, to discover something more of God and what he wants from me. at the moment it doesn't involve completion, but this is the only way I can approach a genuine relationship with him.

I could spend my life content with what is only a lesser reality (maybe this is what we assume "the world" to be, but it could be any pretense we have put up, even close to home) and I would never know him. I know this because a real relationship can happen only between someone who knows himself or herself and the person he or she is relating to. anything less would be not a sincere relationship but a make-believe interaction of acquaintances, not friends or equals. we could never be even remotely equal to God, but somehow we are still meant to be like him.

"restore thine image so much, by thy grace,
that thou may'st know me, and I'll turn my
face" (5.13, Donne).

we talk about knowing God and becoming like him but both are so much more than the things I do or don't do. maturity has to be a holistic maturing not just limited to my spiritual persuasions. it would be in somehow knowing him for who he is and what his purpose is for me, which would require knowing myself to a degree that this purpose could affect me and I could relate back to him. spiritual growth would be as much an awareness of these processes and my environment, emotionally, mentally, and physically, because they too would affect what becomes of me.

self-expression may be seen as a modern trend (5.14, Schaeffer), and maybe this includes self-consciousness because it needs an outlet to get a handle on. but even so it would be a positive trend and too slow in coming.

I sometimes have the idea that all of human history is in some way moving us to a higher degree of self-awareness, and this, if handled correctly, would lead to a heightened sense of awareness of those things beyond our immediate comprehension as well.

even the postmodern period with all of its blurring of elements and stories and ideas could produce an openness to a much greater reality and maybe even to God's purposes, because the only way we could ever access them was through a fragmented perception.

postmodernism sees synthesis and beauty even in disunity, and the child of the kingdom (of all people) should be able to do the same. if not in appreciation at least in faith.

maybe God created us because his own awareness of beauty and truth was so overwhelming that he couldn't keep it to himself any longer, like an artist who bubbles over with desire to communicate to someone else. but God isn't limited to smaller forms like we are.

if he desired at all to create it must be so intensely beautiful as to surpass human imagination. they say that everything was made for his glory, and this has often been presented as a sterile or an unsympathetic thing. but when you have found beauty or created it, you desire to share it with someone else, and maybe he created us to be admirers of this intricacy as well.

and the beauty would somehow be only a token of knowing him.

s i x :
    f a i t h .

never underestimate the power of denial. (6.1, *American Beauty*)

it's funny that I would ever write an apology for faith, seeing as how it has been awkward for me, or an apology for the presence of God, because it feels like I've missed it more often than not.

I need him to be here more than I need the idea that he exists. it isn't much comfort to know that he's out there somewhere if he stays so far away when I need him most.

"these things he said in words. but much in his heart remained unsaid. for he himself could not speak his deeper [fear]" (6.2, Gibran).

I know that he's waiting for me and that he must be watching me, but I wonder if he sees me and I wonder if it would ever make a difference if he did. sometimes I feel him close, but those moments never last and they hurt me more than anything else, especially when they're gone.

it's strange how little of a friend he can be if it's relationship he wants so much from me. I don't know what to make of this, because no friend wouldn't want to be there for another, especially if they needed him. and it seems like he's hardly even there.

we seem to be attracted to people who have the independence to remain distant from us, and I don't know why. I know it's a mistake people who are insecure make, and maybe this means something for knowing God, because none of us could feel secure in relation to him. I wonder if he takes advantage of this or if it keeps us in suspension waiting for him to come close again because we couldn't hold on to him the last time.

they say that we owe God our love because of what he's done for us. but it seems to me that love goes both ways, and it doesn't work if one side decides not to participate one day. if I love someone for what they did for me when I first knew them and not for who they are, I'm just holding on to a ghost. and I'm not sure what he is to me.

faith was always made out to be a natural act, more an aftereffect of knowing God or being known by him. I don't know what this has to do with real life, but I'm sure it works out somehow. Tillich said that faith is "the state of being grasped by an ultimate concern" (6.3), but this seems uncomfortable now and less important than more immediate concerns.

the fundamentals of his existence have never changed as far as I'm concerned. there is little we can know for sure, even in faith. but I know that he exists and that he is everything (but separate), and I know the only way of coming to him is through his son, the savior. I don't think I ever stopped believing this, but he has seemed much more apathetic than I thought he could be.

I tried hard to follow suit, but it came out more like being angry or dejected. and these feelings always have something else behind them. he doesn't have any reasons at all, at least that I know, and I can't let the ones that I have go. sometimes I wish I could hate him, but at least there is something to hate, and some nights this keeps me alive.

maybe this is what faith is.

he doesn't seem too concerned about explaining why his absence feels so strong, and neither does the book, except that it was real to more people than me. how arrogant we are to excuse it away when even David asked God not to hide from him, and so did God's own son when he was dying. obedience wasn't the issue then, and neither was faith, just the reality that he still exists and the reality of all this. nothing was added and nothing was taken away.

we should learn when to be quiet and let things be what they are. they used to say that at the prison where I tutored, but come to think of it that's what they never said. they talked about faith being big enough to move mountains and to get them out of prison, but only one knew better, and he was the only one who wasn't supposed to be there.

"faith is often used as equivalent to confidence," wrote Calvin (6.4). but it's not. even the schoolmaster of predestination realized that we are on the other side looking in (or maybe out), and this leaves us in an awkward position for now.

I used to think that confidence was something that grew stronger as I matured. someday I would hardly question or doubt at all, and I would be calm. but that seemed to be linked more to what I would learn not to do than to anything I would become, or what I knew of God or his promises. I didn't know him like I needed to, and if I'm going to benefit from his promises I need to understand them better too, because they haven't worked yet.

I think I've learned to be quiet for the most part, but I hold a lot in as well. I hate when someone explains this to me without knowing what I think or what I'm afraid of. it's not only arrogant but wrong, because empathy and encouragement are all about understanding where the other person is coming from first.

but I think I am as much a part of the problem as anyone because I don't know myself well enough or especially what someone else could need. sometimes I assume my way right past this, and I know no one needs that. I could just as easily become an atheist and find the same protective emptiness there.

Chesterton said that we care more for consistency than for truth (6.5), and this must be true because consistency is so much easier to manage than truth. it might all come crashing down, but if it comes close to that, we build it up even more with the excuse that it's real truth we are protecting. but real truth never seems consistent. what would it be consistent with? me or everything else I believed?

"there is no truer statement than this: God will not do wrong" (Job 34:12).

I always thought that good hurt less than this. good things have come my way, but not like I expected. the bigger they get the more they seem to be teaching me some kind of lesson instead of making me feel happy or secure. they were always taken away, except for this. (but I don't know how good it is.)

promises of perfect peace or joy or anything you ask for "in my name," and mostly that everything works together for the good, have never made sense to me. and I would almost say they lied if I wasn't afraid of crossing some unspoken line. (I know God doesn't lie.)

I have expectations for how life ought to be, with or without faith, and it's easy to make myself believe that they are promises that God made to me. and I know this because I've done it more times than I want to remember, and I still do, as careful as I try to be. but it is an awful mistake to make.

maybe God is just as disappointed as us, because he knows what it means to be sad. but it must be his only means of waking us up just the same. I would have to let these simple dreams go before I could ever see anything more of what he wants me to see.

"to give up illusions is the condition for giving up circumstances that require illusions" (6.6, Marx).

a teacher said once that he thought he was in the wrong religion if God allowed him, when he was trying his best to please him, to make mistakes. it wouldn't measure up to who God is. I think I understood what he was trying to say, but it didn't come out right.

the prayers to please God and the prayer for wisdom are the ones that are usually answered, maybe even more than others, because they are the most pure. but I don't believe this means we still won't ever make mistakes, even if they are part of the answers.

and I think you should be careful what you pray for.

"because of this I tell you, all things—however stupendous the matters you pray about and request for yourselves—keep believing that you have already received, and consequently it shall be yours" (6.7, Sauer).

most of the time I am a functional atheist. I believe in God, but it's not as if this means much for my day-to-day life. somewhere between this way of functioning and giving up completely, I have moments when I'm able to hope again and I choose to believe that God could help me more than just in the abstract.

I never stopped believing he could help me if he wanted, but I usually don't allow myself to ask.

sometimes I need too much not to and I think I could try one more time. I could have chosen better things to ask for then, but it was too late. it always seems as though God wants us to have faith that he can do or change anything, and really to expect as much. but real faith must be something else, because I've had faith for that before and it never worked, not home, not here, not her (or her), or anything really.

I don't read as much into spiritual leanings as I used to. the last time I did I trusted them more than ever before and allowed myself to go on for months before I fell harder than I ever had. I should know by now that life never ends with any one disaster, but it ended then and it took me a year to get it back.

it seemed like the right thing to have faith in at the time, but I'm still a little confused about the results. I followed my heart and what I thought God was telling me, and I had done this before and hated myself for it, but I kept on hoping because I couldn't turn back anymore and I almost needed to keep hoping more than I needed the answer I was hoping for.

she was an object of my imagination more than a real person, and what I remember of her now is so different from what I wanted her to be then. I wanted someone I had made for myself and I wanted God to help me get her back. I wanted life to go on happily ever after with her by my side, because she could make everything better just by looking in my eyes. and I never expected her to make me whole but I thought she could share what was part of me. it must have been too much to ask, and it turned into more of a disappointment than I felt at the time.

a friend told me once that she used to think words could fix anything, and I thought if not words, maybe love or faith.

I sat in the balcony of a chapel during evening service praying for resolution when I knew I had gone too far. I listened to verses and to songs that made me think that anything was possible if I could only hold on, and they all made me think of her.

I sat there by myself in the dark with my head in my hands and my eyes moist and then I knew that God was there with me. for the first time I sensed that his presence could be something real and that he held me. I could follow the progression of thoughts that ran through my head from knowing he was in this heartache to knowing that good would come of it someday, when he would be even better to me. I sat there entranced with tears streaming down my face. and when the music faded away I felt peace and I knew that he loved me.

I never knew this before.

there are few moments I would point to in my life as genuinely spiritual or when I knew that God really spoke to me, but there was no doubt about this one.

so I forged ahead with my newfound resolution and hope and applied them to my circumstances with every amount of reserve I could muster. sometimes I wished she could know the amount of faith that went into trying to change her, but she never did. not like I needed her to.

I thought it was almost cruel how it all turned out. it felt like betrayal at the time, but I didn't know how much it would hurt me before it was all over. I always thought that somewhere in my longing or in the things he said to me that night was something he wanted to happen.

I wanted it almost as much as I wanted not to need anymore, but he knows what we want even before we ask.

later that semester I decided to pray one last time, but just for an explanation for what had happened. I'm not sure I ever expected him to give me one. a friend said he thought God was proud of how I had held my head up so far, but I just felt like a dog that can't walk away from its own vomit.

I didn't wait for an answer so much as bumble along until it came to me one day. it never really had anything to do with her, or with me, not like I thought it would. it was different than I expected and more some sort of entrance to the part of me that I could never get over. because I allowed myself to forget ever needing her, but I never could forget why.

the same teacher who talked about not making mistakes said that faith isn't something we can hold on to by ourselves or understand for what it is. he was referring to Luther, but the same applies to all of us.

maybe it's doubt when I'm closest to the truth, and real need when I'm nearer to faith than I am to my own misperceptions. if faith is a gift, it must be defined by the one who gives it and not limited to my own mediocre understanding of grace.

maybe he is trying to give himself to me, and some gifts have strings attached. I don't think this makes them any less gifts, but it relates to my acceptance of them.

emphasizing the glory of God is important because it helps us look past ourselves to who he might be. Paul said nothing is as important as knowing him, but I think he meant the reverse of that too. and he said the same about knowing Christ, except that it happens mostly through suffering. I don't know how to feel about this because I prayed that prayer when I was little and I never expected it would be answered this way. maybe a temporary sickness, or some discomfort or change, but not that it would take me completely away from hope or from him and bring me back all the more hurt and uncertain.

suffering doesn't hurt unless I know that it does. and I know my prayer was answered, because I understand this now and I recognize God in a way I didn't before. I know this is a good thing, but it doesn't always feel that way, maybe because I would still never choose to suffer. but I know when it's given to me, and I know it doesn't really matter what I think.

Paul wrote about not being proud of what we can't achieve ourselves, and this would have to fall somewhere under that umbrella too. maybe that's what faith is. and maybe that's what it means to be incomplete.

seven:
the simple life.

> this concerns *us:* setting it all in order
> is the task we have continually before us. (7.1,
> Rilke)

Lewis once said he thought there were people who liked
happiness and people who strangely enough don't (7.2).
I wonder if this applies to a simple life too, or if most of
what I've said implies I don't want it to be simple or
even believe that it could exist.

but contradictory as it may seem I want it very much,
just like I want to be happy. but I don't believe the two
go together anymore and I don't think either were meant
for me. I'm not even sure if they exist (at least as we
know them). but maybe that's just the melancholy
talking.

Barth said that nothing can be "simple and straightforward and obvious" unless it is taken out of its "context and then treated superficially" (7.3). I tend to agree because in my experience nothing is simple unless we choose to make it that way. (when I was a child I thought like a child, and I was supposed to be past this by now.)

simplicity will be possible again when intricacy isn't possible any longer, at least as a complication. and this would rule out life itself, let alone our perception of it. I used to think it could be easy if I believed enough, but I believe more than I did then and it hasn't worked out that way. Jesus said to expect difficulty in this life, but maybe he meant something else because Paul said to let all things work themselves out with God and not to worry.

the farther I go into truth and into my experience of life (I know I'm not supposed to put much stock in this) the more awkward it seems to become. I used to think that writing and reading would help me understand, but I feel like I'm smarter now but not much better off. and I'm not sure I have that much to say.

it seems best to let life happen and do what I can to coexist in some way that seems right, but I'm not always sure if it is. I'm not sure if the guilt I feel when I fall short is real or self-inflicted, because I fail either way.

and if I fail some way today it must just be a little reminder of what it's like to be me all the time.

it's hard to read the book and not be overwhelmed by extremes, sometimes even by ultimatums. if I have any motivation to pursue God seriously, I would have to take each of them seriously, but I did that once and I would have killed myself if I hadn't walked away.

and that doesn't seem right either.

I remember reading how Tolstoy was determined to lead a perfect life (as he thought it was meant to be), but his entire existence testified to how badly he failed, and so did his constant guilt, which made him crawl inside himself for days (7.4, Yancey).

"our whole life is in flat contradiction with all we know, and with all we regard as necessary and right" (7.5, Tolstoy).

they say that ignorance is bliss, and maybe this is what it takes to be less than God. ideals are impossible for anyone to live up to, especially me. it isn't just that I'm weak but that even my perception of them is incomplete. and I don't mean to say that I don't know all of the excuses that could get me past them but that I have no idea how far obedience to them is required.

when we try to live up to them we pick the smallest places to start from because they are the easiest to change. but when we change them it usually ends up being to some extreme much different from the one that was intended, which would be the closest I can ever come to balance.

obedience becomes doing the things I am told to do in sermons and in my new, devotional self-help checklist, and sin becomes actions that we all know are bad. even grace becomes the removal of the consequences of reality if only I can stick to doing what I've been told.

the book says that God reveals truth to the childlike. maybe they understand it because they've always understood things bigger than themselves, at least to let them be. and we're supposed to hold on to this innocence while growing up and learning to interact with bigger things. I'm not sure if I know what spiritual maturity is, but maybe Lewis was right when he said we might not be very close at all (7.6).

the mantra of the Christian life, "trust and obey," is supposed to be the epitome of wisdom and simplicity. but the more I think about it and the more I've needed it to be true, I don't think it means what I want it to.

the problem is that both ideas are inextricably linked to what I think it means to trust and to obey. trust who and what? and what exactly am I obeying? and if my ideas are at all off-base, so will be the consequences. but the consequences are supposedly not up to me. happiness is

not a fish you can catch, no matter how pure your
motivations are.

we have always had a cause-and-effect view of our
relationship with God. and this is unfortunate not only
because it's a misconception of truth (with resulting
mistakes) but also because we're unaware of the position
we were left in to begin with, which would be the
ultimate cause and would never be promising.

we have a mental image (and I think I'm borrowing this)
of moving in and away from God, sometimes building
partial walls to hide parts of ourselves from him. and all
along we have been nowhere and anywhere in the palm
of his hand, and nothing is unseen to him.

I read once that I was supposed to be perfect and
anything less was something I wasn't allowed to be.
(but I knew I was.) I tried so hard to improve but I
wasn't able to change. for a while I thought I could
because it didn't seem so complicated, but then there
were so many smaller things to change that I couldn't
keep track of anymore.

I know now this is what they call obsessive-compulsive
disorder, or maybe legalism, but at the time it just
seemed like the right thing to do.

I read about grace and peace but I didn't think they were
meant for me because they were like prizes for being
complete and I was too hopeless. I even taught about

peace once in a Bible study class, but it was the kind of peace that comes after getting everything right. and I wanted so badly to believe what I was saying but it didn't add up for me.

then I remembered the things I had forgotten and pretended were resolved, ways I couldn't love again and how I couldn't stay away from things that were less. it wasn't long before I knew this better and I thought it would be easier to give up than to keep trying. it was too hard, and faith wasn't worth it if it was going to be part of the failure too.

I told God that if he was who he claimed to be then he could bring me back someday when things were better. two years later he did, but not to perfection but to a new perspective on the same mistakes. and I thought this was strange but I finally accepted that it could be true, because some things run deeper than the surface.

(it took me much longer to realize that this had anything to do with hurt.)

a few years later I saw how a Victoria's Secret model (the picture, not the model) and one of my less dignified sexual experiences eventually brought about two of the most healing moments ever in my life, and both with someone real. I don't know how that could happen or how most of the good in my life seems to come despite being myself or something worse.

and I want to go about things differently next time, not just for my sake but because it makes him smile. but in the meantime God must be big enough to work good of even my biggest mistakes (because somehow most of my life falls into this category), and he lets them lead me on to something better, which is where I still need to be.

I think this must be what grace is, a gift of his embrace even when I'm at my worst, which must seem to be all of the time to him. we think that the farther we go into the spiritual life the more we will fit the mold of someone who has the right to be here. but our position was always a gift to begin with and nothing is changed about that now. we're still little children, but at least we have a place to belong.

Chesterton said "we are not altering the real to suit the ideal. we are altering the ideal: it is easier" (7.7). I know there's some truth in this, especially when it's easier to be content than to change. but there's only so much I can change, and what I do comes back anyway. I can never change the tendency to fall back on myself.

everything about me seems weak, not just my thorn in the flesh (whatever that is limited to). I wish it wasn't this way because I see the mess it makes of my life and in my relation to everyone else. I want to go away like I did before, because I don't want to try anymore. but I withdraw just as much from life as I do from myself.

I can't even pretend like I used to. the constant effort to hold back the part of me that never falls in place became too much one day and I didn't have the energy left to hide it. but it was almost a relief to finally accept it, and it's the closest I've come to any kind of resolution (never release).

94 "every actual entity is an integration of opposites—inner plus outer, past plus future, self plus other" (7.8, Grenz, Olson).

Chesterton also said that Christianity was the first belief to state that ethics aren't manageable in balance, like the pagan (or even the modern) world thought, but only in "the collision of two passions apparently opposite" (7.9). Paul said we are never free from the conflict between what we want and what we know is good. we're always somewhere in the middle.

and this is what it means to be human, even a new creation.

ethical perfection is like the idea that there should be no pain in the world or doubt, but all of these things belong to a reality that isn't complete yet.

"ethics, like the kingdom itself, stand in the tension between present realization and future eschatological perfection" (7.10, Ladd).

eschatological tension (the tension of the end days) is what dr. Pate meant when he said that the end of this age has come (7.11). the age to come dawned with the coming of Christ but it won't be complete until he returns. and nothing in this in-between time will be either. each of us thinks we can become one of the few exceptions, but that kind of perfection is just as small as the problems I have limited it to.

Ladd said that many of the laws the Jews thought they had under control individually became much more inclusive when Jesus spoke about them. hatred became murder and lust became adultery, because they were just symptoms of deeper issues, and deeper issues can't be controlled by laws because they belong to the heart (7.12). and who could control a heart or cut it up and manage the pieces independently?

the process of education, both in and outside of school, is intended to bring a child to maturity by giving him or her the tools to cope with all of life as an adult. we forget, especially in the church, that one of the biggest parts of this is bringing a child from a concrete to an abstract level of understanding; from numbers and letters, and shapes that fit into puzzles, to things that aren't contained in objects.

to enter the kingdom of God you are required to understand sin and faith and salvation, and all of these are abstract concepts but presented as concretes, which is necessary for someone simple to understand. even big ideas should be able to be explained as something small so that even the most uneducated can approach them.

I don't know if we ever get any closer to God, but this is always where we leave off.

we forget sometimes that the kingdom is of the heart, and this must be the hardest for us to understand because he allows us to orient it on our own toward him. some things he wants not to be owed but actually given.

the book says we have the mind of Christ and even the Spirit of God inside, but these are just beginnings too. he sees our hearts and also our inability to understand his bigger purposes, and the greatest difficulty is in allowing both realities to continue and to know that he has a purpose for this as well.

somehow the approach or the effort must be worth more to him, at least for the moment, than what we were meant to become. maybe because they require dependence from me when I would save myself, or maybe because they are a choice I would rather not make.

some of the strongest warnings are directed at trying to secure a different position.

"have you lost your senses? . . . why are you now trying to become perfect by your own human effort? . . . are you now going to just throw it all away?" (Gal. 3:3–4).

we are eternally in the business of re-creating what was given to us. of course we can be most defensive here because it seems like we're pursuing holiness. but we've made too many mistakes going after one extreme of it or another when we were meant to let it be what it is.

"the kingdom of God isn't ushered in with visible signs. you won't be able to say, 'here it is!' or 'it's over there!'" (Luke 17:20–21).

we made the biggest mistake in thinking it was ours when even God never gave it to us completely.

I used to think this might be an excuse to accept the things that I know are half, and then I imagined it would limit the possibility for fulfillment in this life, like I thought when I was little. I understand this better than I did, but I still haven't come to terms with it completely. I do know it's better to accept what I've been given and hope that it will grow than to make something of what isn't there. whatever is left undone is better than what was never started at all, and they always said to look for God where he's at work.

we spend most of our lives hiding from ourselves and hiding from God and anyone else who could take anything from us, because we have nothing to give.

"both the creation of an idealized image and the process of [displaying it] are attempts at repairing damaged self-respect, but . . . both only injure it still further" (7.13, Horney).

there is a maxim that says it's not what you do but who you are that matters. maybe all he wants is for us to admit to what's already there, both in recognition and in the desire for that dim image to clear, and that just in becoming genuine we have shown ourselves to be real friends.

98 "just as all ethical interaction consists of becoming apparent before God" (7.14, Kierkegaard).

then maybe we can get somewhere.

e i g h t :
    h e a l i n g .

sometimes God takes his beauty back, for now.

most of what we do is in response to fear, either that we will be hurt again or that the effort won't be worth the disappointment after all. even when we try for something good or something higher it's usually just to protect ourselves from something worse, like guilt or hopelessness, and sometimes even need.

I don't know if this is not such a bad thing or if it's just another excuse for failure. we love only because we know what it is and we want more of it. if we are ever friends with God it must be so he can give us something we can't give ourselves, and I'm not sure what he gets out of it. maybe he gives enough so we would never leave. but that sounds like codependency, and I know he doesn't need me. and I think he gave me most of the things I want to give away.

I want to be better now.

(I think this is the part I wanted to write the most.)

I wrote in my notebook a year ago that I wanted to write because I needed to know what prayer God answers anymore, if he does at all. I knew that he is good and that he listens, but I didn't know if my prayer meant anything to him or if it was just a way of falling in line with what he was doing already.

there is so much I need and so much I still want, but I don't know if it matters as much to him as it does to me. I've learned to push it under and try to pretend I never wanted it in the first place. then if it happens it was meant to be and if it doesn't I won't be disappointed. but I still am.

need is heavy enough to carry around without wondering if it will ever be answered.

we're told not to demand miracles from God but never to stop asking, because one day some of them will be given away and maybe even here. but I think so less and less.

"for if the powers of the kingdom are present and active because the kingdom is thought to be very near when in fact the kingdom is not near at all, then the message of . . . the powers of the kingdom must itself be illusory, for it rests upon an illusion" (8.1, Ladd).

thy kingdom come, thy will be done, on earth as it is in heaven. his will seems to have everything to do with me and nothing at all with what I wanted. all I want from him is simple peace and maybe just a few days to be happy. I even ask for it now and then, but I'm afraid when I feel it coming because I don't know how it will be taken away. most of all I want to be free from all this, because it changed from a book I was writing with some kind of answers to something that is still able to drown me.

(not in beauty, like I thought at first, though it seems to play along.)

I wasn't sure if I would make it through this, and there were moments when even getting it out didn't seem like enough reason to stay. I would lie there and stare at the ceiling, wondering how it could hurt so much to exist. maybe there was some purpose in sleeping so I could record the nightmare tomorrow for someone who hurts just as much. but if the dream never ends there comes a point when you wonder what was so special about it to tell on.

I went to church on new year's eve and saw a clear moon on my way home and I thought it was just like before when I knew God was with me. I prayed the *kyrie eleison* and thought it could make a difference this year, and not because it had to (I know better now) but maybe because it could.

I don't know if there is an end to this, except that somehow life goes on and I can't be done with it until it's finished with me (8.2, Kierkegaard). there's something I still need to do, and sometimes I think maybe I just need to stick around until it happens to me.

I don't know what to ask for anymore, but they tell me that God knows this and that he's already answered my unspoken prayers just like the ones I did say out loud. I think I know better what not to ask for now, and I know more of the things I shouldn't expect to be good to me. I know so many that I don't know if any healing ones are left. I know the things that hurt and the mistakes I shouldn't ask for help with again, but I don't always know whose fault they were. sometimes I take too much responsibility for life.

is there something I still don't see, something so important that everything else will wait until I see it?

I'm not sure I can wait much longer, and soon this will be done.

"I consider it a dangerous misconception of mental hygiene to assume that what man needs in the first place is equilibrium or, as it is called in biology, 'homeostasis' . . . a tensionless state" (8.3, Frankl).

102   the longing for completion must be the ultimate tension (and temptation), but what if healing wasn't the end of that tension or maybe even a lessening of it but the full absorbing of the tension and a lifetime lived with it? we have a distorted idea of healing because we think that something must have ended for it to take place.

but the only way for that to happen now would be for me to leave, because some things will not be over until I do.

the book says all of creation was placed under the curse of incompletion and it's still waiting for the day when it will be free from decay.

"but if we look forward to something we don't have yet, we must wait patiently and confidently" (Rom. 8:20).

Richard Haarden, a mixed-media artist, said once that Christian visual art is so weak, just like our music and literature, because we try to say too much at once instead of allowing truth to develop. I think God allows parts of a greater whole to linger, but we are not as patient with ourselves. we need time and permission to process where we are before we can move on. and we certainly don't process anything all at once. if we did it wouldn't be pretty and we could never accept it. we'd have to see it as a much hazier picture.

"Freud insisted that mental health was not a simple matter of healthy vs. diseased, but more of a continuum. he saw no clear line of demarcation between emotionally healthy and emotionally sick persons" (8.4, Shenk).

I wonder what it feels like to be well. I see happy people all around me and I wonder what it's like to be one of them, and to smile. I feel them staring at me as if it's strange that someone else could live in such a different place, but they never ask me why. and when I tell them, it always comes out wrong, like when I try to write.

I feel like I'm defending someone I used to be or who I am to them, and not what I really am now or who I will be someday. I'm not sure they can be separated like that or if it only happens when I talk to others. they say it helps to forget things, but there's so much to remember and some of it makes me smile and some of it still makes me hurt, but it's all part of a story that might mean more to someone else than it does to me.

some people let go of the past so much that they lose themselves today. and I ask them what happened to them or why they act like they do now, and they can't make a connection between the two, or they just don't tell me. some disappointments are meant to be shared, if only with myself, because somewhere in the piecing back together they could turn out to be part of something whole.

it's the ones I can't forget because they come back every day that I have a hard time processing. I could keep everything in the open and still not be prepared for them, but they don't seem so strange at least. months from now or maybe even in a couple of weeks I might be able to see them as something better, but right now they just hurt.

I've tried to write them off as stupid and immature or something I will regret crying over later. but this doesn't take away the tears in my eyes as I fall asleep.

"let me say I believe God will supply all my need, and then let me run dry, with no outlook, and see whether I will go through . . . , [or] sink back to something lower" (8.5, Chambers).

faith is awkward like that. I think the answers it gives keep me afloat more than comfort or relieve anything. maybe that's a pessimistic thing to say, but it's not just me who hurts. what about those who are sicker or maybe even waiting for death? they don't just "get better," and you don't tell them they should be over it by now.

grief doesn't count for much with most of the church (or society as a whole), and neither does psychological illness, which is strange because the church still suffers the most from both. we make the mistake of thinking bad things happen only to others, and when they happen to us (God forbid) they're nothing a little biblical counseling or stress relief can't fix. psychology is a form of complicating the issue without bringing anything spiritual into the equation, but our form of counseling is empty of anything human except for the recognition of universal sin, which is of course the grand resolution for need.

I heard someone say once that the world is full of orphans, and this must be true. no one should go without love, whether it was never given or it can never be felt for some reason. sometimes I think this hurts most of all. but I wonder if this teaches me what I wouldn't have known any other way, like emptiness that's bigger than the things I try to contain it in and a need that's bigger than not being alone.

they say we hurt so we can empathize with someone who feels the same way. but I listen and sometimes I can even give a little bit, but I can never love enough to take anything away.

sometimes I wonder if God can either, because I ask him to take the pain away but he never does. if he died to take away our sin, he must not be so concerned about everything else. but even that's not gone. Paul prayed three times for his thorn in the flesh to be removed and

God never did. (sometimes you can pray more than three times.)

they told me to give everything to him and let him carry it, but I think he holds me while I hold the hurt.

"come to me, all of you who are weary and carry heavy burdens, and I will give you rest" (Matt. 11:28).

the closer I get to him the more it hurts to be me even if I know better what it's like for it to be well with my soul.

it's funny how that happened, but I think it's the only peace I have. it would be hard if it was taken away again.

I saw a little girl holding the hand of a beautiful woman, and the little girl was just as beautiful except for the birthmark or scar that covered the side of her face. I thought it was brave how calmly she walked in a store full of people, and the look of tired determination on her mother's face showed how she carried her daughter's pain and maybe much more.

I thought about what the little girl must be thinking, how people look at me funny, but it doesn't matter because my mother is holding my hand. and I know I am different and other children laugh at me, but it doesn't matter because right now my mother is holding my hand and they can't hurt me. and I thought about how God sits next to me and sometimes I reach for his hand, but it doesn't matter because he holds mine anyway. and sometimes this isn't enough because I'm not a child anymore, but it doesn't matter because I will always be his little boy. I ask him why he doesn't speak more or why when he does it sounds so unfeeling to me. but I think he said that he would rather be quiet because I can't understand what he wants to say, and silence usually means that someone is sad.

how have we made God a curse on anyone who hurts? we remember him well enough and even the cross, but we forget what it's like to feel alone.

Nouwen wrote some of the most sympathetic material on the struggles of the Christian life. he wrote some of the most meaningful and encouraging words you could ever imagine, but Yancey says he was one of the most tormented people alive. he described him as "a deeply insecure person of anguish, pain, and craving" and said he battled his whole life with not just emotional wounds but sexuality as well.

being a priest he never allowed himself to act on the homosexual urge, but he never stopped fighting it or working it out "in terms of restlessness, loneliness, and rejection," and he took all of them with him to his grave (8.6). we don't know how this could be true, and if it is there must be something wrong with what he said. but we never understand that his insecurities could have been the very things that gave him empathy or even wisdom, until they happen to us.

Cobb said that we can love only when we know that we have been loved in our own weakness, and we can accept ourselves only when we know we don't need to save ourselves any longer (8.7).

any salvation that needs to happen is already in progress, and for now it's from my ideal of the way things should be.

"it was only *sickness* that brought me to reason" (8.8, Nietzsche).

and this can happen only when I am in the middle of losing my ideal and staying where I am so I can be part of the process, because otherwise it would be happening to someone else or I would be some other place, which would defeat the purpose.

I won't be someplace else until later. dr. Pate said sometimes the things we think will end up killing us become the things God uses to work the biggest miracles in us. Paul wrote that he was completing the suffering of Christ when he hurt, for the good of the kingdom. I don't know how this could be, but Christ said we could achieve even greater things than he did, and his mode of operation almost always involved incompletion, if not pain.

acceptance is a strange thing. it's necessary in order to function with any amount of sanity in life. but it could also be just an excuse for letting things continue as they are, for better or for worse, when I know well enough they should be better. I just don't know how much of a difference I can make.

it's not that the paradox or the intricacy is so unsettling, because it doesn't take much effort not to think about it at all. but I know that if I try it will require some kind of change that will be uncomfortable, and I'm not sure I can do that. it must not be right somehow.

"the good taught you false shores and false securities: you were born and kept in the lies of the good" (8.9, Nietzche).

in acceptance is peace, but I've seen this amount to resignation or ignorance and mostly fear. you could stand up to everything in life and know hardly a moment's rest but still accomplish more good than if you watched it pass by or caved in on yourself. I thought that happened only to people who thought too much, but you could hardly accuse most of us of that.

we settle for wristbands and pop imitations and play catch up to the rest of social reconstruction. Horney wrote that some people expect "to do away with the harmful consequences of . . . unresolved conflicts without changing anything in the conflicts themselves—an attitude characteristic of every neurotic attempt at solution" (8.10). of course some things can never be changed completely, and incompletion might be the biggest one of all.

but I know this by now, and I know it's no excuse not to try. Jesus never stopped fighting against the things in his power to affect, no matter their priority or the result. maybe the effort is just as important as success because at least I am reaching. I could wait for perfection to come and not know half of what I was meant to learn in the meantime, that there is more to this life than accomplishing what I thought I needed to.

n i n e :
h o p e .

> what we cannot reach flying we must reach limping. . . . the book tells us it is no sin to limp. (9.1, Rückert)

I have been writing for eight months now and have spent every one of them waiting for the day when I will be done and this part of my life will be over. now that I'm here I'm not sure what's left, which is a strange thing for a twenty-four-year-old to say.

I've been so focused on finishing this, and not because writing a book is so important anymore but because it's everything I haven't been able to let go of. and I still want it to be over, but not as much as I want it to mean something.

sometimes you have to create good; it doesn't always come of itself. and even when it does it's always slow in coming. I think maybe it passed me along the way, because it wasn't waiting for me now that I'm done. I think I'm more proud of having survived than having created anything, and that has more to do with everything I remember and everything still in store than with anything now. but maybe that's all right.

I don't know what comes next, but I hope it's good.

Tolstoy said that living is an act of worship (9.2), and I wonder sometimes about this. I wonder if life is ever more than the sacrifice of everything I thought to be good, which seems to happen without my trying to, or if there's something meant to be meaningful, maybe even beautiful, in the experience itself.

I think of sacrifice and I think of losing everything, but maybe that's because I don't know enough yet to look past this. maybe there is something in the experience worth just as much as what I will be given at the end, and maybe as much as what I could ever lose here. Christ said that if you give your life away it will come back to you even more, but if you try to keep it you will have lost it anyway.

112 "nothing in the universe can be the same if somewhere, we do not know where, a sheep that we never saw has—yes or no?—eaten a rose.... look up at the sky, ask yourselves: is it yes or no? has the sheep eaten the flower? and you will see how everything changes" (9.3, *The Little Prince*).

maybe this is as good as it gets, and that would be a strange thing, and it's not at all what I expected to say.

I can choose to step back or I can choose to stay, and it has been more of a daily decision than the resolution I made last spring. I used to think that all I studied and learned would someday make me impervious to any difficulty life could throw at me, maybe even hurt. I knew this wouldn't happen, but I didn't know how much the other extreme could be true. I feel both wiser and more insecure than I did then, and I feel I'm not much closer to what I needed to say. but I know I am.

I'm afraid of letting it be what it is, which is only the beginning of something else. but I know that it is what it was supposed to be. I didn't know that when I began, and I couldn't have expected this. I expected it to be much more hopeful and complete, but I don't know if it would have been better that way.

it wouldn't have been sincere.

a lot of what I studied confirmed what I believed in the first place, mostly the essential doctrines of the faith, but at the same time that those essentials can be that much more disturbing. I'm not sure if what I learned makes anything easier, but maybe it will after the fact. or maybe to someone else.

I keep thinking about the verse that says when we've done all he has asked of us we will receive everything that he promised. I've thought about that a lot the past year, and I'm not sure that it helps much.

I know what the promise means on the other side, and when I started to write I thought I would put a lot more emphasis on that. eternity is the whole other half of the tension or paradox, but maybe I chose to concentrate on the part that shows itself here because it's all I really can do. I still don't know what the promise means on this side, if anything. I think it just means that God is here with me in the middle of it, whether I feel him or not. and that may sound cliche, but that's all I can say.

Robert McAfee Brown wrote that "those who hope for hope—after an eternity—are entitled to do so only if they have measured that which has the power to obscure hope, only if they have lived in the shadow of utter denial" (9.4).

the same friend who showed me what beauty is told me that maybe the people who need and want the most in this life will see their desires met that much more on the other side. then maybe all of this was meant for me not just to wait for them but to fuel my desires even more. and maybe in some awkward way this is where I find God, because it means I haven't given up on finding an answer yet.

someday all of the other things will be gone and mostly hope, because I won't be waiting anymore. for now I'm tired, but I think I might be done for tonight.

"dream my heart away one endless night, one
          foggy day
gaze into a blue so clear
void within my head of noise, but peace
dreaming for that someday I'll be through with
          here" (9.5).

t h a n k s .

115

to dr. Pate for exposing me to a thesis that was captivating and healing at the same time (at least a little bit), and mostly for allowing me to hurt.

to Brian for pulling something out of the manuscript that was worth the loyalty and attention he gave to it, even when there was a lot working against us, including my own ignorance and compulsiveness.

to Stan, Lyn, and Jen and the rest of Zondervan for taking a chance with this one and putting a whole lot of quality into it once they did.

to Kim for closing the deal.

to Common Children for inspiring the title.

to my parents and grandparents for many things.

to Chuck and Stephanie for making it possible for me to survive my first year out of school.

to Janet, my manager, for endless encouragement and flexibility.

to Karen and the rest of the design room for watching over their prodigal son and always asking for an update.

to Barb and Bruce for a place to stay and a car to use while I waited for a contract.

to Caribou Coffee Gurnee and Vernon Hills (especially Shawn, Owen, and Ryan) for a place to write and a whole lot of free coffee.

to Carol, Jess, Krista, Ingrid, Shannon, Andy, Pam, and Christine for their friendship, reviews, and help with many practical things.

to Jay for the mentorship and a really optimistic handshake.

to Dave for showing me that the manuscript could be relevant to a world slightly larger than my own and for many valuable long talks.

to Scott for taking me under his wing and standing by each step of the process as if it was his book.

to Cheryl for her companionship and support from the very awkward beginning.

notes.

preface.

(0.1) Ben DeVries, "Words." © 2002 by Ben DeVries.

(0.2) Rainer Maria Rilke, *Letters to a Young Poet,* trans. M. D. Herter Norton, rev. ed. (New York: Norton, 1954), 89.

(0.3) Lewis Carroll, *Alice in Wonderland* (Old Saybrook, Conn.: Konecky and Konecky, n.d.), v.

one: between.

(1.1) Author's paraphrase of John 17:15–16 NLT.

(1.2) C. Marvin Pate, *The End of the Age Has Come: The Theology of Paul* (Grand Rapids: Zondervan, 1995), 11.

(1.3) Cleanth Brooks, "The Language of Paradox," in *John Donne's Poetry: Authoritative Texts Criticism,* ed. A. L. Clements (New York: Norton, 1966), 178.

(1.4) Thomas Aquinas, *Summ. Theol. Ia Q XXV Art. 4,* quoted in C. S. Lewis, *The Problem of Pain* (New York: Touchstone, 1996), 23.

(1.5) Oscar Cullmann, *Christ in Time: The Primitive Christian Conception of Time and History,* trans. Floyd V. Filson (Philadelphia: Westminster, 1950).

(1.6) Ben DeVries, "delicate fade." © 2002 by Ben DeVries.

two: sorrow.

(2.1) Lewis Carroll, *Alice in Wonderland* (Old Saybrook, Conn.: Konecky and Konecky, n.d.), 3.

(2.2) Alastair Hannay, introduction to *Either/Or: A Fragment of Life,* by Søren Kierkegaard, ed. Victoria Eremita, trans. Alastair Hannay (New York: Penguin, 1992), 15.

(2.3) Benedict J. Groeschel, CFR, *Healing the Original Wound: Reflections on the Full Meaning of Salvation* (Ann Arbor: Charis/Servant, 1993), 11.

(2.4) Albert Camus, *The Myth of Sisyphus,* quoted in Jeanette Hardage, "The Art of Story: A Conversation with Walter Wangerin, Jr.," *Mars Hill Review* 19: 51–64.

(2.5) E. L. Doctorow, *City of God* (New York: Plume, 2001), 212–13.

(2.6) Rainer Maria Rilke, *The Selected Poetry of Rainer Maria Rilke,* ed. and trans. Stephen Mitchell (New York: Vintage, 1989), 65.

(2.7) Ben DeVries, "Delicate Fade." © 2002 by Ben DeVries.

(2.8) Viktor E. Frankl, *Man's Search for Meaning,* rev. ed. (New York: Washington Square, 1985), 115.

(2.9) Thomas Aquinas, *Summa Theologica,* SMT FP Q[2] A[3]R.0.2 Para 1/1, Reply OBJ2.

three: beauty.

(3.1) Leo Tolstoy, *The Kingdom of God Is within You: Christianity Not as a Mystic Religion but as a New Theory of Life,* trans. Constance Garnett (Lincoln, Neb.: University of Nebraska, 1984), 117.

(3.2) Nine Inch Nails, "Leaving Hope," *NIN Live: And All That Could Have Been,* disc 2 (Nothing, 2002).

(3.3) C. S. Lewis, *The Weight of Glory,* rev. ed. (New York: HarperCollins, 1980, 2001), 30.

(3.4) G. K. Chesterton, *Orthodoxy: The Romance of Faith* (New York: Image/Doubleday, 1990), 54.

(3.5) Susan A. Stein, *Van Gogh: A Retrospective* (St. Paul, Minn.: Beaux Arts Editions, 1986).

(3.6) Søren Kierkegaard, *The Sickness unto Death: A Christian Psychological Exposition for Upbuilding and Awakening,* ed. and trans. Edna H. Hong and Howard V. Hong (Princeton, N.J.: Princeton, 1980).

(3.7) Rainer Maria Rilke, *The Selected Poetry of Rainer Maria Rilke,* ed. and trans. Stephen Mitchell (New York: Vintage, 1989), 249.

(3.8) Kierkegaard, *Sickness unto Death,* 30.

(5.3) C. S. Lewis, *The Problem of Pain* (New York: Touchstone, 1996), 87.

(5.4) Benedict J. Groeschel, *Spiritual Passages: The Psychology of Spiritual Development,* rev. ed. (New York: Crossroad, 2000), 185.

(5.5) Stanley J. Grenz and Roger E. Olson, *Twentieth-Century Theology: God and the World in a Transitional Age* (Downer's Grove, Ill.: InterVarsity, 1992), 191. The authors are summarizing theologian Wolfhart Pannenberg's thinking.

(5.6) Deftones, "Change (in the House of Flies)," *White Pony* (Maverick, 2000).

(5.7) Augustine, *City of God,* quoted in Benedict J. Groeschel, CFR, *Healing the Original Wound: Reflections on the Full Meaning of Salvation* (Ann Arbor: Charis/Servant, 1993), 24.

(5.8) Sigmund Freud, *Beyond the Pleasure Principle,* trans. James Strachey (New York: Norton, 1989), 63.

(5.9) Bishop Kallistos Ware, *The Orthodox Way,* rev. ed. (Crestwood, N.Y.: St. Vladimir's Seminary Press, 1995), 73.

(5.10) Lewis, *Problem of Pain,* 18–22.

(5.11) Frederick Buechner, *The Hungering Dark* (San Francisco: HarperSanFrancisco, 1985), 14.

(5.12) "God not only foresaw the fall of the first man, and in him the ruin of his descendants, but also meted it out in accordance with his own decision." John Calvin, *Institutes* (3.23.7).

(5.13) A. L. Clements, ed., *John Donne's Poetry: Authoritative Texts Criticism* (New York: Norton, 1966), 92.

(5.14) Francis A. Schaeffer, *How Should We Then Live? The Rise and Decline of Western Thought and Culture* (Old Tappan, N.J.: Revell, 1976), 158.

six: faith.

(6.1) *American Beauty* (DreamWorks, 2000).

(6.2) Kahlil Gibran, *The Prophet* (Teddington, Middlesex: Senate, 2002), 7.

(6.3) Paul Tillich, *Biblical Religion and the Search for Ultimate Reality* (Chicago: University of Chicago, 1955), 51.

(6.4) John Calvin, *Institutes*, 3.2.

(6.5) G. K. Chesterton, *Orthodoxy: The Romance of Faith* (New York: Image/Doubleday, 1990), 28.

(6.6) Karl Marx, quoted in Erich Fromm, *On Being Human* (New York: Continuum, 1999), 41.

(6.7) Translation of Mark 11:24 by Dr. Ronald Sauer, Moody Bible Institute.

seven: the simple life.

(7.1) Rainer Maria Rilke, *The Selected Poetry of Rainer Maria Rilke,* ed. and trans. Stephen Mitchell (New York: Vintage, 1989), 73.

(7.2) C .S. Lewis, *The Weight of Glory,* rev. ed. (New York: HarperCollins, 2001), 10.

(7.3) Karl Barth, *The Epistle to the Romans,* trans. Edwyn C. Hoskyns from 6th ed. (New York: Oxford University), 425.

(7.4) Philip Yancey, *The Jesus I Never Knew* (Grand Rapids: Zondervan, 1995), 136–42. Philip Yancey, *Soul Survivor: How My Faith Survived the Church* (New York: Doubleday, 2001), 119–46.

(7.5) Leo Tolstoy, *The Kingdom of God Is within You: Christianity Not as a Mystic Religion but as a New Theory of Life,* trans. Constance Garnett (Lincoln, Neb.: University of Nebraska, 1984), 115.

(7.6) Lewis, *Weight of Glory*, 105–6.

(7.7) G. K. Chesterton, *Orthodoxy: The Romance of Faith* (New York: Image/Doubleday, 1990), 106.

(7.8) Stanley J. Grenz and Roger E. Olson, *Twentieth-Century Theology: God and the World in a Transitional Age* (Downer's Grove, Ill.: InterVarsity, 1992), 131. The authors were writing in reference to process theology.

(7.9) Chesterton, *Orthodoxy,* 92.

(7.10) George E. Ladd, *The Presence of the Future: The Eschatology of Biblical Realism,* rev. ed. (Grand Rapids: Eerdmans, 2000), 292.

(7.11) C. Marvin Pate, *The End of the Age Has Come: The Theology of Paul* (Grand Rapids: Zondervan, 1995).

(7.12) Ladd, *Presence of the Future,* 292.

(7.13) Karen Horney, M.D., *Our Inner Conflicts: A Constructive Theory of Neurosis* (New York: Norton, 1992), 151.

(7.14) Thomas C. Oden, ed., *Parables of Kierkegaard* (Princeton: Princeton University, 1989), 129.

eight: healing.

(8.1) George E. Ladd, *The Presence of the Future: The Eschatology of Biblical Realism,* rev. ed. (Grand Rapids: Eerdmans, 2000), 130.

(8.2) Thomas C. Oden, ed., *Parables of Kierkegaard* (Princeton: Princeton University, 1989), 85.

(8.3) Viktor E. Frankl, *Man's Search for Meaning,* rev. ed. (New York: Washington Square, 1985), 127.

(8.4) David Shenk, *The Forgetting: Alzheimer's: Portrait of an Epidemic* (New York: Doubleday, 2001), 76.

(8.5) Oswald Chambers, *My Utmost for His Highest* (New York: Dodd, Mead, and Co., 1935), 242.

(8.6) Philip Yancey, *Soul Survivor: How My Faith Survived the Church* (New York: Doubleday, 2001), 301–3.

(8.7) John Cobb, *The Structure of Christian Existence* (Philadelphia: Westminster, 1968), 135.

(8.8) Friedrich Nietzsche, *Ecce Homo: How One Becomes What One Is,* trans. R. J. Hollingdale (New York: Penguin, 1992), 26.

(8.9) Ibid., 99.

(8.10) Karen Horney, M.D., *Our Inner Conflicts: A Constructive Theory of Neurosis* (New York: Norton, 1992), 61.

nine: hope.

(9.1) Rückert (translation of one of the *Maqâmât* of al-Hariri), quoted in Sigmund Freud, *Beyond the Pleasure Principle,* trans. James Strachey (New York: Norton, 1989), 78.

(9.2) Leo Tolstoy, *The Kingdom of God Is within You: Christianity Not as a Mystic Religion but as a New Theory of Life,* trans. Constance Garnett (Lincoln, Neb.: University of Nebraska, 1984).

(9.3) Antoine de Saint-Exupéry, *The Little Prince* (New York: Harcourt, 2000), 91.

(9.4) Robert McAfee Brown, introduction to *Night,* by Elie Wiesel (New York: Bantam, 1982), vi.

(9.5) Ben DeVries and Cheryl Hudgin, "Momentary Dream." © 2000 by Ben DeVries and Cheryl Hudgin. Used by permission.

We want to hear from you. Please send your comments about this book to us in care of zreview@zondervan.com. Thank you.

ZONDERVAN™

GRAND RAPIDS, MICHIGAN 49530 USA

WWW.ZONDERVAN.COM